THE PROFESSIONAL EDUCATION OF TEACHERS

Second Edition

The Professional Education of Teachers:

A Humanistic Approach to Teacher Preparation

Arthur W. Combs
Robert A. Blume
Arthur J. Newman
Hannelore L. Wass

University of Florida, Gainsville

Allyn and Bacon, Inc. **Boston**

470 ATLANTIC AVENUE, BOSTON, MASS. 02210

Second printing September 1974

LIBRARY OF CONGRESS CATALOG CARD
NUMBER: 73–85718

PRINTED IN THE UNITED STATES OF AMERICA.

Contents

Preface

Some improvements in education can be brought about by spending more money, by building better schools, and by introducing new courses of study, new standards, or new equipment. But the really important changes will come about only as teachers change. Institutions are made up of people, and it is the behavior of teachers in classrooms that will finally determine whether or not our schools meet or fail to meet the challenge of our times. It is at the source of supply—in our teacher-preparation programs—that major efforts must be directed if we are to bring about the improvements we need in education.

Many efforts at reform of teacher education have resulted in little more than a reshuffling of the same old courses, a heavier load of content for teacher-education students, and some changes in procedures for certification and licensing of teachers. This is not enough. Teacher education needs much more than a tinkering job.

These are exciting times in the social sciences. Beginning about 1940 a whole series of new concepts about man and his behavior appeared on the scene. This social science breakthrough has resulted from the emergence in American psychology of a great new humanistic force, a new psychology deeply concerned with people, values, perceptions, and man's eternal search for being and becoming. The impact of these new ideas is powerful indeed. They promise new solutions to age-old human problems. Already they have profoundly influenced the work of several other professions. Little by little as they find their way into education, they promise similar revolutions for teaching and learning. Where these ideas will eventually lead us no one can say, but this much is certain: No profession charged with responsibilities for human welfare will ever be the same for, whenever our ideas about the nature of man change, great changes are called for in the ways we live and work with people. This is especially so for teaching, the most human profession of all.

This book is an attempt to translate what some of the basic concepts of modern perceptual-humanistic psychology seem to mean when applied to the problems of teacher education. We have not attempted to design a comprehensive teacher-education program. That is a local problem to be worked out by particular faculties charged with teacher-education responsibilities. Instead, we have tried in this book to look at the professional aspects of undergraduate, preservice teacher education through a new set of lenses provided by perceptual psychology in an attempt to establish new guidelines for both teachers and students involved in teacher education. Seen in this way, some traditional practices are corroborated; that is comfortable. Some long-held traditions are also brought into question; that is distressing. Most important of all, new directions are suggested promising much for the future, and that is exciting!

The first edition of *The Professional Education of Teachers* grew out of two major resources: (1) a series of researches on the nature of the helping professions carried out at the University of Florida over a ten-year period; and (2) a number of basic principles from modern humanistic psychology applied to the problems of teacher education. It was intended as a kind of position paper for teacher education and both the author and the publishers expected a limited distribution among teacher-educators. Much to their surprise the book was an immediate success, requiring a series of rapid reprintings to keep up with demand. Apparently, it filled a need, not just for professional teacher-educators, but as an introductory text for students just entering the profession of teaching as well.

Immediately after publication the author was also besieged by requests from teachers' colleges for the services of persons trained in the kind of program it outlined. At first this was most embarrassing for the author had to reply that the program he outlined in the first edition did not exist on his own campus either! But in 1967 this changed, as a group of the faculty of the College of Education at the University of Florida met to design a New Elementary Program using the guidelines expressed in *The Professional Education of Teachers*. This program was placed in operation side by side with the existing program and a research design was formulated to provide a disciplined evaluation of outcomes. The NEP thus represents a unique development in teacher education: a perceptually oriented program for the education of teachers (1) based on fundamental research, (2) developed into a theoretical position, (3) placed in actual operation, and (4) researched to determine its effectiveness. To this point it has attracted much national and international attention especially for its humanistic orientation. It has also proven an exciting and stimulating experience to the staff and students involved in its formulation and development since 1968. In addition, feedback from the students now out in the field as full-time professionals and first results from research indicate the program may, indeed, be on a better track.

The original researches on which *The Professional Education of Teachers* was based have been considerably expanded since 1965. New studies have been completed at the University of Florida on student teachers, "master teachers," and junior college teachers. A further series of studies has been completed at the University of Northern Colorado dealing primarily with college teaching. All these results tend to corroborate and extend the earlier findings on which *The Professional Education of Teachers* was established.

This second edition attempts to update the content of *The Professional Education of Teachers* in light of the above developments in research and practice. To accomplish this the original author invited three persons intimately associated with the New Elementary Program and its assessment to contribute their experience and thinking to this revision. We have also agreed to address this second edition to students entering the teaching profession as well as to their instructors. This represents, in part, an adjustment to the widespread use of the first edition as an introductory text for teachers. It is also consistent with the authors' firm belief that the education of a teacher is a process in personal becoming. This calls for the deepest possible involvement of beginning teachers in every aspect of their professional education and the use of their own experience as a laboratory for the development of their own unique style of working with students.

To this end our revision has addressed itself to the following questions:

1. What makes a good teacher?
2. What do these concepts mean for student teachers?
3. What do they mean for program developers?
4. In conclusion, we include a short description of how one institution goes about solving these problems.

The authors wish to publicly recognize three groups of people who contributed greatly to the production of this book:

First, we wish to extend our thanks to the students and faculty with whom we have worked in the University of Florida New Elementary Program. The development of the NEP provided an invaluable laboratory within which it has been possible to test our concepts in daily interaction with a truly remarkable group of people as stimulating and exciting as any we have ever known. In a very real sense this volume is as much their book as ours.

Second, we are keenly aware that the freedom to innovate provided by our colleagues and the administration in the development of the New Elementary Program here at the University of Florida is all too seldom seen in college circles. We are doubly grateful, therefore, for the opportunities the faculty and administration of our college and the university have provided us to experiment with an entire teacher-education curriculum. The support and encouragement they have given our efforts at curriculum reform have made it possible to test our theoretical postulates in practical operation of a teacher-education program.

Finally, we wish to extend our warmest thanks and appreciation to the office staff of the Childhood Education and

Foundations of Education Departments and especially to Mrs. Elsie Voss for assistance in the preparation of this manuscript far beyond the call of duty.

Arthur W. Combs
Robert A. Blume
Arthur J. Newman
Hannelore L. Wass

1

What Is a Good Teacher?

Whatever we do in teacher education must depend on having an accurate idea of the nature of good teaching. That seems clear enough. How to arrive at such definitions, however, has proven a most difficult problem. Despite millions of dollars and millions of man-hours poured into research on the problem over the past fifty years, the results have continued to be frustrating and disappointing—until recently.

It now appears that our failure to find useful definitions may be due to the fact that we have been looking for answers in the wrong places. For several generations teacher-education programs have operated with a concept of good teaching derived from the mechanistic view of behavior characteristic of American psychology during the past fifty years. Now a new psychology has appeared on the scene that shifts our understanding of behavior from a mechanistic to a humanistic view. Applied to the problem of good teaching, this new frame of reference seems to provide us with better answers to old questions. To put the matter in perspective, let us begin with a look at some earlier attempts at defining good teaching.

THE TEACHER AS KNOWER

The earliest conception of the good teacher was that of the scholar. It was assumed that a person who knew could teach others. Of course it is true that a teacher has to know something, but even without research it is apparent to anyone who looks that knowing is simply not enough. Most of us can recall out of our own experience the teacher who "knew his subject but couldn't put it across." Sometimes there can even be found good teachers whose depth of information in a particular field is woefully lacking. This is often shocking to some critics of education who still equate teaching with scholarship. One study has demonstrated that *both* good teachers and bad ones knew equally well what a good teaching situation *ought* to be like![1] Knowing is certainly important to teaching, but it is clear that good teaching involves much more.

THE "COMPETENCIES" APPROACH TO TEACHING

The second approach to defining good teaching has been in terms of teacher "competencies." The thinking goes something like this: If we know what expert teachers do, or are like, then we can teach beginners to be like that. This is a straightforward, uncomplicated approach to the problem and seems logically sound. The idea has produced great quantities of research into the traits of good teachers and their methods.

Research on Specific Competencies

This has provided us with long lists of competencies supposedly characteristic of good teachers. In the beginning these lists were simple. Since what people do is always related to the situations they are in, every situation calls for a different behavior and the more situations the researchers examine, the longer the lists of competencies have become. As a consequence, these first attempts to describe the competencies of good teachers specifically yielded few useful results. In 1959 the American Association of School Administrators commissioned a team to review the research on good teaching, hoping to find some guidelines to the practical decisions about teacher quality necessary in carrying on their jobs. Sadly, the team was forced to report that apparently there is no specific trait or method exclusively associated with good teaching.[2]

Research on General Competencies

Some investigators have thought better discriminations might result from studying the general, rather than the specific, traits or methods of good teachers. Approaching the problem in this way, they have been able to find fairly stable distinctions in such general terms as good teachers are "considerate" or "child-centered" or "concerned about structure." One of these, for example, is a study by Marie Hughes[3] under a grant from the United States Office of Education. Dr. Hughes developed an exhaustive system for analyzing teacher behavior and applied it to time-sample observations of teachers in the classroom. She was able to demonstrate a number of general classes of behavior seemingly characteristic of good teachers. Among these were such categories as controlling, imposition, facilitating, content development, response, and positive or negative affectivity. Similar attempts to analyze teacher behavior have been carried out by Flanders,[4] Smith,[5] Bowers,[6] Filson,[7] and Medley.[8] These examinations of the more general aspects of effective teaching have been somewhat more successful in discriminating between good and poor teaching than research on specific behavior or methods. But they still do not provide us with the definitive distinctions needed by the profession. Good teaching, it is clear, is not a direct function of general traits or methods. Summing up the situation, a noted educator has concluded, "It is commonplace, but not very flattering to this commentator, to deplore the fact that more than half a century of research effort has not yielded meaningful, measurable criteria around which the majority of the nation's educators can rally."[9]

Some Practical Difficulties of the Competencies Approach

The attempt to educate teachers utilizing the competencies approach runs into some very knotty problems. In the first place, it is a fallacy to assume that the methods of the experts either can or should be taught directly to beginners. It is seldom that we can determine what should be for the beginner by examining what the expert does well. One of the authors had this clearly demonstrated some years ago when he was given the responsibility for teaching failing university students more effective methods of study. At first glance it would seem logical to teach failing students the study habits of successful ones. Such an approach to curriculum construction, however, is disastrous! When one examines the study habits of successful students, one is likely to find that they study most whimsically. They operate without plan, go to the movies often, indulge in all sorts of extracurricular activities, and generally behave in ways that would be suicidal for students teetering on the brink of failure. It simply does not follow that what is good for the expert is good for the novice too. Nor is it true that the way to become expert is to do what the expert does.

Some of the methods used by the expert can only be used *because* he is expert. Experienced teachers have generally learned to deal with most classroom disturbances by ignoring them. But beginners cannot ignore them! The expert is able to ignore matters precisely because he *is* expert. The attempt to use methods without understanding may only serve to turn the young teacher loose in the blackboard jungle to fight for his life with weapons he does not really know how to handle.

The most recent variation of the competencies approach grows out of the current fashion to demand that all aspects of education define objectives in clearly measurable behavioral terms. This behavioral objectives-performance-based criteria approach to planning and evaluating schooling seems logical and straightforward. It has served us well in spurring production of goods in our great industries and is now being applied to education in the hope it may prove equally effective in the production of intelligent human beings. In teacher education it results in attempts to define "teacher acts" and, thereafter, to teach young teachers to behave in those ways. One such program has defined several thousand more or less specific behaviors expected of student teachers and utilizes giant computers to keep track of their proper completion.

Confronting long lists of competencies is likely to be deeply discouraging and disillusioning to the young teacher. Evaluations of "goodness" or "badness" become attached to methods, and students thereafter are expected to judge their adequacy in these terms. The net effect is to set such impossible goals of excellence that no one can ever hope to reach them.

Discouraging and disillusioning as the behavioral objectives-competencies approach is for the young teacher, it has equally unhappy effects on the older ones. A vast complex of competencies, all of which are demanded as criteria for good teaching, leaves the individual defenseless before criticism. No matter what he does well, it is never enough! There is always so much more that he might have done, or should have done, that he can rarely find pleasure or satisfaction in his accomplishments. Add to this the fact that many of the competencies demanded do not fit the particular personality and so could probably never be achieved anyhow, and the defeat of the individual becomes almost inevitable. In time, the feeling of inadequacy produced by continual failure to meet impossible goals undermines professional pride and is likely to produce a guilt-ridden teacher suffering from a secret feeling of being "too little and too late." It should not be surprising if after years of this kind of experience the will to try shrivels and dies.

THE PERSONAL CHARACTER OF GOOD TEACHING

The Teacher as a Person

As we have seen, research on competencies has been unable to isolate any common trait or practice of good teachers. But this unanimous failure in itself demonstrates an important fact: A good teacher is primarily a unique personality. If good teachers are unique individuals, we can predict from the start that the attempt to find *common uniqueness* would be unlikely to get results.

A good teacher is first and foremost *a person*, and this fact is the most important and determining thing about him. He has competence, to be sure, but not a common set of competencies like anyone else. Some years ago, one of the authors visited a well-known demonstration school. Each classroom had a carefully picked teacher. While he was visiting the rooms in this school with the principal, he was much impressed with the beautiful work that many of the students had produced. Classroom after classroom was charmingly and artistically decorated wih the children's productions: artwork, science demonstrations, biological specimens, collections of all sorts and descriptions. After five or six such rooms they entered another very different from the others. This room was nearly bare of the materials seen in the others. Instead, in this class the teacher sat in the middle of a group of children holding a quiet discussion. Leaving the room with the principal, the author remarked on this fact and was struck by the principal's reply. "Yes," she said, "and you know, I believe that is perhaps my very best teacher. She is not like the others. You can see that. But she gives those children something special. What that girl can do to help children explore an idea is simply out of this world!" Here was a teacher making full and effective use of herself in her own special ways. Fortunately, she had a principal who recognized her genius. It is probable that many a less understanding person would have condemned her for her "obvious inadequacies" as compared to other teachers in the same building.

The personal character of good teaching can be documented by almost any of us from our own experience. If one thinks back to his own school days, he will probably remember that the good teachers he had did not all behave alike or even with great similarity. Rather, each stands out as a person, an individual, some for one reason, some for another. Each had his own peculiar methods, values, and techniques. Good teaching is like that, an intensely personal thing.

The Uniqueness of Methods

One may often hear teachers speak of "good" or "bad" methods of teaching. Actually, the methods good teachers use are so infinitely varied as to defy rigid classification into such neat categories, and research on good teaching has generally been unable to isolate any specific method invariably associated with either good or bad teaching. What teachers mean when they speak of "good" and "bad" or "right" methods are those they have found effective and consistent with their beliefs about the proper goals of education.

The good teacher is not one who behaves in a given way. He is an artist, skillful in facilitating effective growth in students. To accomplish this he must use methods appropriate to the complex circumstances he is involved in. His methods must fit the goals he seeks, the children he is working with, the philosophy he is guided by, the immediate conditions under which he is working, to say nothing of his own feelings, goals, and desires. He may even, on occasion, find himself using a method he believes is "bad" because at that moment it was the only thing he could think of to deal with an emergency situation.

The description of methods or competencies as "good" or "bad" in themselves is much too simple. The methods we use must take into account people, situations, and purposes. The same criteria cannot be applied equally to the beautiful school in the wealthy suburb and the dingy school in the slum. Though its methods may be different, the school in the slum could be doing a better job, given its particular problems and situations, than the wealthy school in the suburb. The development of students and the growth of intelligence and personality are the goals we seek, and whether these are being achieved or not cannot be determined by focusing exclusively on a study of the methods employed in the achievement of such ends.

THE "SELF-AS-INSTRUMENT" CONCEPT

The shift in our thinking from a mechanistic to a personal view of teaching is by no means confined to our profession alone. In fact, most other professions dealing with human problems have preceded us in this direction. The effective professional worker is no longer regarded as a technician applying methods in a more or less mechanical fashion. We now see him as an intelligent human being using himself, his knowledge, and the resources at hand to solve the problems for which he is responsible. He is a person who has learned to use himself as an effective instrument. In medicine, this principle finds expression in the "problems approach" to training. In social work, it is found in the concept of supervision. Modern nursing has adopted a human-relations approach to patient care. Counseling and psychotherapy stress the philosophy of the counselor and the importance of his own personal therapy. These professions do not seek the production of automatons. They want creative, thinking human beings able to use themselves as refined and trustworthy instruments for dealing with complex problems.

The good teacher is no carbon copy but possesses something intensely and personally his own. Artists sometimes call this "the discovery of one's personal idiom." The good teacher has found ways of using himself, his talents, and his surroundings in a fashion that aids both his students and himself to achieve satisfaction—their own and society's too. We may define the effective teacher formally as *a unique human being who has learned to use himself effectively and efficiently to carry out his own and society's purposes in the education of others.*

For the student entering the profession the "self-as-instrument" concept requires that his education be regarded as a problem in becoming. Becoming a teacher is not a matter of learning how to teach. It is a question of personal discovery, of learning how to use one's self well. No teachers' college can make a teacher. The best it can do is provide students with problems, resources, information, and opportunities to explore what they mean. Beyond that the student is his own pilot and must find his own best ways of working. He must make a commitment to the process of learning. After all, the self is unlikely to change if it is not permitted to "get in the act."

If we adapt this "self-as-instrument" concept of the professional worker to teaching, it means that teacher-education programs must concern themselves with persons rather than competencies. It means that the individualization of instruction we have sought for the public schools must be applied to these programs as well. It calls for the production of creative individuals, capable of shifting and changing to meet the demands and opportunities afforded in daily tasks. Such a teacher will not behave in a set way. His behavior will change from moment to moment, from day to day, adjusting continually and smoothly to the needs of his students, the situations he is in, the purposes he seeks to fulfill, and the methods and materials at his command.

How shall a teacher-education program produce such a person? To answer this question we need a frame of reference about the nature of behavior and learning on which to base our thinking and a more precise look at the "self-as-instrument" concept of good teaching.

ENDNOTES

[1]A. W. Combs and D. W. Soper, "The Helping Relationship as Described by 'Good' and 'Poor' Teachers," *J. Teacher Ed.* 14 (1963): 64–68.

[2]W. J. Ellena, M. Stevenson, and H. V. Webb, *Who's a Good Teacher?* (Washington, D.C.: American Association of School Administrators, N.E.A., 1961).

[3]Marie M. Hughes, *Development of the Means for Assessing the Quality of Teaching in Elementary Schools*. Report of Research, Cooperative Research Program, Project no. 353 (Washington, D.C.: U.S. Office of Education, 1959).

[4]N. A. Flanders, *Teacher Influence, Pupil Attitudes and Achievement: Studies in Interaction Analysis*. Final Report, Cooperative Research Program, Project no. 397 (Washington, D.C.: U.S. Office of Education, 1960).

[5]B. Othanel Smith, "A Concept of Teaching," in *Language and Concepts in Education* (Chicago: Rand McNally, 1961).

[6]N. D. Bowers and R. S. Soar, *Studies in Human Relations in the Teaching-Learning Process*. Final Report, Cooperative Research Program, Project no. 469 (Washington, D.C.: U.S. Office of Education, 1961).

[7]T. N. Filson, "Factors Influencing the Level of Dependence in the Classroom," Unpublished Ph.D. Thesis (Minneapolis: University of Minnesota, 1957).

[8]Donald M. Medley and Harold E. Mitzel, "A Technique for Measuring Classroom Behavior," *J. Ed. Psych.* 49 (1958): 86–92.

[9]N. Fattu, "A Profession Seeks to Guarantee the Competence of Its Members" in *New Horizons in Teacher Education*. Report of the National Commission on Teacher Education and Professional Standards (Washington, D.C.: N.E.A., 1964).

2

A Perceptual View of Effective Teaching

If the "self-as-instrument" concept of the professional worker is valid, then teacher education must result in the production of that kind of self. To provide the guidelines for such a program we need to know (1) the nature of the self, (2) how it develops, (3) how it may be changed, and (4) what a good teaching self is like; we need a "self" psychology on which to base our operations. Humanistic-perceptual psychology supplies us with just such kinds of understanding. This way of looking at people and their behavior is different from the psychology most of today's teachers and teacher-educators grew up with.

Present-day teacher education is still deeply influenced by the stimulus-response (S-R) approach to human behavior characteristic of American psychology for fifty years. When it first appeared on the scene many educators embraced it wholeheartedly, hoping it might provide the basis for a scientific approach to problems of teaching and learning. But this hope has given way to disappointment as it has become clear that so mechanistic a view of psychology cannot supply the answers we need. As American education has become increasingly child- or student-centered, the approach to human behavior characteristic of stimulus-response psychology has proven less and less adequate in enabling teachers to carry out their tasks. A whole new practice has arisen calling for new theoretical concepts, new understandings, and new directions.

Theory and practice in human experience do not always develop concurrently. Rather, progress seems to be characterized by a kind of leap-frog operation in which first one, then the other, steps into the lead, each building on past achievements. Sometimes theory moves ahead of practice, sometimes practice outruns theory. So it is in the relationship between psychology and teaching.

THIRD-FORCE PSYCHOLOGY

The Emergence of Third-Force Psychology

Three great movements have characterized American psychology since 1900. The earliest of these was stimulus-response psychology, which originally grew out of attempts to apply the new techniques of the physical sciences to problems of human behavior. Its greatest effect on education in particular came in the 1920's and 1930's: It was then that educational psychology came into being and that the ideas of stimulus-response psychology began to be applied to educational problems. For a while the application of these ideas to teaching-learning problems proved helpful and stimulating. But S-R psychology was not an unmixed blessing; its essentially mechanistic character served to lead the profession down some primrose paths from which many are still unable to turn. For more than a generation best teaching practice has outrun the contributions of stimulus-response psychology as teachers everywhere have discovered more humanistic approaches to learning.

Following World War I, American psychology was caught up in a second great movement, largely stimulated by

Freud and his followers. The effect of this psychoanalytic movement was to turn the attention of many psychologists to problems of human behavior outside the laboratory, and they began to search for the causes of behavior in the life history of the individual. This was really an extension of the S-R approach: It included not just immediate stimuli but the whole gamut of experiences to which a person had been subjected in his lifetime. Looking at man in this way provided useful clues for dealing with many of our educational problems. It still does, but the S-R and psychoanalytic psychological viewpoints are objective, descriptive ways of looking at behavior and lead to mechanistic and atomistic ways of working with people that are often not acceptable in modern practice. Over the years American education has moved increasingly toward a more humanistic philosophy which finds expression in practices designed to facilitate and assist learning rather than to control and direct it. We have outrun traditional psychologies; modern educational thought and practice calls for new understandings of behavior more adequate to deal with our current problems. We need a new psychology to help us with these matters.

Fortunately that psychology is at hand. A new Third Force in American psychology has appeared on the scene since the late 1940's. Psychologists involved in this movement are called by many names. In the group may be found personalists, humanists, self psychologists, phenomenologists, perceptual psychologists, transactionalists, existentialists, and a number of others. All have in common a deep concern with questions of man's being and becoming. They take a view of behavior that is highly consistent with the experience of superior teachers: It is a point of view that sees people as growing, dynamic organisms. It regards human beings not as things to be made or molded but as unique events in the process of becoming. The impact of this new psychology is being felt everywhere in those professions having to do with the growth, development, and welfare of people. It has tremendous importance for education. In particular, it provides the framework for a "self-as-instrument" approach to teacher education.

THREE BASIC PRINCIPLES OF PERCEPTUAL PSYCHOLOGY

For those readers not familiar with the perceptual approach to psychology, let us briefly review three of its basic principles having to do with perception, the self-concept, and the nature of human need. While a high degree of similarity exists in the basic points of view of Third-Force psychologists, it should be understood that there are also important differences among them. The principles presented below are drawn from the brand of Third-Force psychology called "perceptual psychology." They would probably be acceptable to many other Third-Force psychologists, but not to all. For the reader who would like to explore these concepts more deeply, a selected list of references has been included at the end of this chapter.

The Perceptual Basis of Behavior.

The basic concept of perceptual psychology is that all behavior of a person is the direct result of his field of perceptions at the moment of his behaving. More specifically, his behavior at any instant is the result of (1) how he sees himself, (2) how he sees the situations in which he is involved, and (3) the interrelations of these two. When a person sees himself as a student, sitting in a classroom, taking directions, and responding to the teacher's questions, he behaves like a student. A teacher sees himself as a teacher and behaves like a teacher—giving directions, taking responsibility for moving the class along, and helping students to solve problems. Each behaves in terms of what seems to him to be appropriate for the kind of person he sees himself to be in the situation he is in at that moment. The immediate causes of behavior are to be found in the perceptions existing for the behaver at the moment of acting. This seems like a simple, acceptable notion that fits very closely with our own experience.

Perhaps it is precisely because it fits so closely and comfortably that it is often overlooked. One's own perceptions of events seem so "right" and so certain that one is likely to jump to the conclusion that the way one sees things is the way things are. Our own perceptions have such a feeling of reality that when others do not see things in a similar fashion we are likely to jump to either of two conclusions: They are frightfully stupid for not seeing correctly, or else they are perversely trying to annoy and confound us! It is probable that such failure to understand how things seem to other people is the most persistent source of difficulties in human relationships, not only between individuals, but between groups in our society, and between nations.

To understand human behavior, the perceptual psychologist says, it is necessary to understand the behaver's perceptual world, how things seem from his point of view. This calls for a different understanding of what the "facts" are that we need in order to deal with human behavior: it is not the external facts that are important in understanding behavior, but the meaning of the facts to the behaver. To change another person's behavior it is necessary somehow to modify his beliefs or perceptions. When he sees things differently, he will behave differently.

This change in our frame of reference for understanding people brings about a thorough revision of our thinking about many problems of human behavior and interaction, and many psychologists regard it as one of the great breakthroughs of the social sciences. Perceptual psychology has already had profound effects on other professions like social work, counseling, the ministry, and psychotherapy. It is having equally profound effects on the work of many teachers.

Teacher education today is being urged to establish clear, concise behavioral objectives, base certain competencies on them, and test for their attainment. In this way, we are told, the public and the profession can be sure that our new teachers will be competent to teach. For several generations we have been preoccupied with the competencies approach to teacher education with its emphasis on teaching teachers how they *ought* to behave. Perceptual psychology, however, tells us that behavior is only a symptom, the surface manifestation of what is going on within the individual. To attack behavior directly is to deal with symptoms rather than causes, and a symptomatic approach to human behavior is no more likely to be permanently effective than a symptomatic approach to health. Teaching people to behave differently at one time cannot be counted on to affect their behavior at another. They are able to practice the "correct" behavior only as long as they can concentrate on doing so, which is not very long. The realities of life in the classroom are so demanding and so diverse that such concentration cannot long be maintained. Perhaps this explains why so much of what we teach in teacher-preparation programs is slow to find its way into actual practice of the new teacher in the classroom.

If behavior is a function of perception, it follows that teacher education must concern itself with the inner life of its students. Simple exposure to subject matter or teaching methods is not enough. The maturation of an effective professional worker requires changes in the student's perceptions —his feelings, attitudes, and beliefs and his understandings of himself and his world. This is no easy matter, for what lies inside the individual is not open to direct manipulation and control. It is unlikely to change except with the active involvement of the student in the process. Just as children are more likely to learn most effectively if they are actively involved in the process, so, too, effective teacher education calls for involvement of the student teacher in the process.

The Self-concept and Behavior

Of all the perceptions existing for an individual, none are so important as those he has about himself. Each of us has thousands of ways in which he sees himself and each of these has more or less importance in a given personal economy. A person might see himself as a man, husband, father, psychologist, professor, as middle-aged, a resident of Florida, an American, able to swim but not to play polo, adequate to teach personality theory but not statistics, and so on. These and thousands of others make up the peculiar organization that seems to him to be his "very self." It is this organization of ways of seeing self that the perceptual psychologist calls the self-concept. It represents the most important single influence affecting an individual's behavior.

The individual's self is the center of his world, the point of origin for all behavior. What he believes about himself affects every aspect of his life. We now know that many academic deficiencies can be traced to unfortunate concepts of self. For example, most children who come to reading clinics do not come because they have anything wrong with their eyes. The children who come to the reading clinic are, almost without exception, unable to read because they *believe* they cannot read. That is to say, they have developed *concepts of themselves* as people who cannot read. They are prisoners of their own unfortunate self-perceptions. Similar deficiencies in other subjects can be traced to children's ideas about themselves as unable to spell, unable to write, unable to do algebra, or whatever. In adulthood people may suffer from feelings of being unable to make a speech, dance, or do arithmetic. Millions of people are victims of the beliefs they hold about themselves.

The effect of the self-concept extends far beyond the matter of skills, however. We now know that even an individual's adjustment or maladjustment is likely to depend on the ways in which he perceives himself. The psychotherapist knows that the maladjusted persons with whom he works are people who characteristically see themselves as unliked, unwanted, unacceptable, unable. On the other hand, adequate, effective, efficient, self-actualizing, well-adjusted citizens are persons whose self-concepts are highly positive. They perceive themselves to be persons who are liked, wanted, acceptable, able. They see themselves as belonging, responsible, effective personalities, and, because they see themselves so, they behave so. Teachers, too, are affected by the adequacy of their self-concepts.

The self-concept is not something a person is born with. It is something each of us learns as a consequence of his experience with those who surround him in the process of his growing up. We *learn* that we are men or women, able or unable, acceptable or unacceptable, liked or unliked, depending on the kinds of experiences we have had in the process of growing up. Once established, the concepts we have of ourselves continue to affect our behavior, perhaps even for life.

All this means that teacher education must be deeply concerned about the developing self of the fledgling teacher. How a teacher behaves after he leaves the portals of his college will be very largely determined by how he has learned to see himself and his relationships to his students, his subject matter, his administrators, and to the profession of teaching itself. Teacher education must thus become as student-centered as we have hoped the teachers we are currently producing would be in their own classrooms. To provide a frame of reference for the construction of its curriculum it also needs the most accurate understanding of the kinds of self-perceptions associated with effective teaching. We will return to this point later in this chapter.

The Basic Need for Personal Adequacy

The most important thing about man is his existence, the fact of his being and becoming. Modern psychology sees man as engaged in a continuous striving for self-fulfillment. In this process each of us seeks by every means he can to be "enough," not just for the present but for the future as well. The basic need for personal adequacy thus includes both striving for self-maintenance and for self-enhancement. It is not the physical self each of us seeks to maintain, however. It is the self of which we are aware, our *self-concepts*, we seek fulfillment for. Even behaviors that at first glance seem to be self-destructive turn out to be self-maintaining or enhancing when they are seen from the point of view of the individual. So it is that the hero may give himself up to certain death rather than see himself as a coward or a traitor to his fellows. In our own experiences we often place our physical selves in jeopardy for the sake of enhancing our concepts of self. For example, we drive too fast, eat too much, work too hard, even when we know better.

The need for adequacy is the fundamental motivation of every human being from conception to death. It provides the drive toward health and mobilization of the body's resources to resist the attacks of disease. And it causes the client in psychotherapy to move toward better adjustment and personal development when he is helped by the therapist to remove the blocks that lie in the path of his recovery. The drive toward health does not have to be learned; it is a characteristic of life itself and provides the motive power for every human act.

This drive has tremendous implications for education. Its existence means it is not necessary to motivate people—a problem with which we have often struggled. Everyone is *always motivated* to be and become as adequate as he can be in the situations as he sees them. Students may not be motivated as their teachers would like, but they are always motivated in terms of their own basic need.

Knowledge of this innate drive changes the whole structure of the educative process from that which our ancestors felt was essential. If people are always motivated to become as adequate as they can, they are seeking the same goals for themselves that their teachers ought to be seeking for them! The task of the teacher is not one of prescribing, making, molding, forcing, coercing, coaxing, or cajoling; it is one of ministering to a process already under way. The role required of the teacher is that of facilitator, encourager, helper, assister, colleague, and friend of his students.

In the pages that follow we have attempted to point out some of the implications these principles of perceptual psychology have for teacher-education practices. Before we turn to that question, however, we need to look more closely at the "self-as-instrument" concept of teaching. If the effective use of self-as-instrument is to become the goal of teacher education, we need to define more precisely what kind of self that is.

THE SELF-AS-INSTRUMENT CONCEPT

In recent years a number of psychologists have been examining the nature of the helping relationship.[1,2] One of the most interesting of their findings is that helping relationships, wherever they are found, seem to have a high degree of similarity. These kinds of relationships are to be found in many places and in many kinds of settings created by many different kinds of people. Wherever they are found, however, they seem to have certain common characteristics. That is true in the classroom, the counseling office, in psychotherapy, or in the relations between teachers and supervisors, supervisors and principals, or administrators and staff.

In one study a number of psychotherapists from different schools of thought were asked by Fiedler[3] to describe what they considered to be the elements of an ideal therapeutic relationship. He found that experienced therapists from different schools of thought were in greater agreement about the nature of the helping relationship than were beginning and expert therapists of the same school. Apparently, no matter what the school of thought from which these therapists began their work, as they grew more experienced they came to see the helping relationship in highly similar terms. Even more surprising, when Fiedler asked "the man in the street" to describe the nature of a good helping relationship, he found that the ordinary citizen described it about as well as the experts! It would appear from this that there is such a thing as a "good" human relationship, and that all of us, professional or not, as a consequence of our experience are able more or less explicitly to recognize it when we meet it.

Several years ago one of the authors became intrigued with these results. He wondered if the helping relationship as seen by good teachers would agree with the relationship as seen by expert psychotherapists. Accordingly, he and one of his colleagues applied Fiedler's helping relationship Q-sort to a group of superior teachers in a university laboratory school. Sure enough, the good teachers were in close agreement with the expert therapists about what a helping relationship ought to be like.[4] They next applied this instrument to two groups of "very good" and "very poor" teachers selected for them by students and supervisors.[5] They expected to find considerable differences; but quite the contrary, they found poor teachers could describe the good helping relationship just as well as the good ones. Apparently everyone knows what a good helping relationship *ought* to be even if he cannot produce it.

Psychologists who have been investigating the nature of the helping relationship are unable to define it on the basis of specific things which helpers *do*. They can, however, discriminate between good helpers and poor helpers on the basis of their perceptions. When we look at the question of what helpers do, we find that they behave in hundreds of diverse ways, among which there seems to be no common characteristic. When, however, we look at the perceptual organization, or belief system, of helpers we begin to find important differences between good helpers and poor ones. For example, it has been found that helpers can be distinguished from nonhelpers on the basis of their attitudes, feelings, and purposes and their conceptions of themselves and others.[6] Since good teaching is also a kind of helping relationship, these findings suggest again the importance of a perceptual approach to teacher-education programs.

THE PERCEPTUAL VIEW OF EFFECTIVE TEACHING

The need to take a perceptual view of teacher education has already been suggested by other writers.[7,8] It is the basic thesis of this book. *Whether an individual will be an effective teacher depends fundamentally on the nature of his private world of perceptions.* It follows that the perceptual world of the student must be a matter of vital concern to teacher-education programs.

At the University of Florida we have been wrestling with the question: "What kinds of perceptions do 'good' professional workers have?" Our studies began with a year-long seminar devoted to the question in 1960. Out of this study we developed a series of hypotheses which we thought were probably characteristic of good professional workers.[9] Since then we have been engaged in a series of researches designed to measure whether our beliefs about good professional workers' perceptions were really so. To this date we have been able to test our hypotheses on counselors,[10] Episcopal priests,[11] and several varieties of teachers.[12] These results have been further corroborated in a series of researches at the University of Northern Colorado.[13] In each instance our hypotheses have been verified to an extent even we were unprepared to expect.

As a consequence of these studies we have come to believe that the following major areas are crucial in the perceptual organization of a good teacher:

1. Rich, extensive, and available perceptions about his subject field.
2. Accurate perceptions about what people are like.
3. Perceptions of self leading to adequacy.
4. Accurate perceptions about the purpose and process of learning.
5. Personal perceptions about appropriate methods for carrying out his purposes.

The Good Teacher Is Well Informed

The good teacher is not ignorant. He has a rich, extensive, and available field of perceptions about the subject matter for which he is responsible. This is the aspect of teacher education on which everybody agrees: Teachers should be knowledgeable people. What is often not understood by many critics of modern education is that teachers rarely fail because of lack of knowledge of subject matter. When they fail it is almost always because they have been unable to transmit what they know so that it makes a difference to their students.

It should be clearly understood that the perceptual view of teacher education considers this "knowing" phase to be of first-rank, though not exclusive, importance in the professional education of teachers. Generally speaking, we have done much better with this phase of teacher education than with any other. Therefore, if the matter seems to be given less emphasis in this book than other aspects of teacher education, this is not because it is less important, but only because it is less in need of attention. "It is the squeaky wheel that gets the grease."

Accurate Perceptions about People and Their Behavior

Teaching is a human relationship. To behave effectively good teachers must possess the most accurate understandings about people and their behavior available in our time. Each of us can only behave in terms of what he believes is so. What a teacher believes, therefore, about the nature of his students will have a most important effect on how he behaves toward them. If a teacher believes his students have the capacity to learn, he will behave differently from the teacher who has serious doubts about the capacities of his charges. The teacher who believes his students can learn begins his task with hope and assurance that both he and his students may be successful. He can place confidence and trust in them and be certain that if he is successful in facilitating and encouraging the learning process they can, they *will*, learn. The teacher, on the other hand, who does not believe his students are capable approaches his task with two strikes against him. If you do not believe that children can learn, it is surely not safe to trust them.

A series of researches at the University of Florida and the University of Northern Colorado investigated the perceptual differences between good and poor professional workers in teaching, counseling,[14] and the ministry.[15] From these studies, it appears that good teachers can be clearly distinguished from poor ones with respect to the following beliefs about people:

Internal-External Frame of Reference. The good teacher's general frame of reference can be described as internal rather than external; that is to say, he seems sensitive to and concerned with how things seem to others with whom he interacts and uses this as a basis for his own behavior.

People-Things Orientation. Central to the thinking of the good teacher is a concern with people and their reactions rather than with things and events.

Meanings-Facts Orientation. The good teacher is more concerned with the perceptual experience of people than with the objective events. He is sensitive to how things seem to people rather than being exclusively concerned with concrete events.

Immediate-Historical Causation. The good teacher seeks the causes of people's behavior in their current thinking, feeling, beliefs, and understandings rather than in objective descriptions of the forces exerted upon them now or in the past.

Teachers need a clear and consistent frame of reference about people and their behavior to serve as a guide in dealing with them. This need not be a formal psychology represented by a particular school of thought, but it must be as accurate and true-to-life as possible. False beliefs about the nature of people can only result in the selection of inappropriate ways of dealing with them. The good teacher's psychology must be more than accurate, however. It must also be a point of view to which the teacher is deeply committed, for without personal involvement no point of view has any significant effect on behavior. It is a personal psychology which the good teacher needs, derived from accurate observations and given consistency and meaning by personal exploration and discovery. A prime function of the teacher-preparation program must be to assist its students in the development of such a frame of reference for their future behavior.

Perceptions about the Self

The behavior of a teacher, like that of everyone else, is a function of his concept of self. Teachers who believe they are able will try. Teachers who do not think they are able will avoid responsibilities. Teachers who feel they are liked by their students will behave differently from those who feel they are disliked. Teachers who feel they are acceptable to the administration can behave differently from those who have serious doubts about their acceptability. Teachers who feel their profession has dignity and integrity can behave with dignity and integrity themselves. Teachers who have grave doubts about the importance and value of their profession may behave apologetically or overly aggressively with their students and with their colleagues.

It is apparent that if the self-concepts a person holds about himself are as important in determining behavior as modern psychology suggests, then teacher-educators must be deeply concerned with the kinds of self-concepts students are developing. This is comparatively new ground for the teacher-education program. Teaching subject matter has always been a recognized task. Even teaching psychology has long been accepted as a responsibility. But few teacher-educators so far have given much thought to incorporating good self-concept development in their programs. A self-as-instrument approach to teacher education must assign this question a high priority. We need to seek from research workers much more information about the kinds of self-perceptions characteristic of good teachers. And we need to examine teacher-education curricula and practices with an eye to their effects on the self-concepts of students.

Perceptions about the Purposes and Process of Learning

Behavior always has direction. Whatever we do is always determined by the purposes we have in mind at the time of our behaving or misbehaving. What teachers perceive to be their own and society's purposes makes a great deal of difference in their behavior. The teacher who believes that schools exist only for the able and that "it is a waste of time to fool with the poorer students," behaves differently from the teacher who perceives society's purpose as helping all children become the best they can. Similarly, what teachers believe about how students learn will markedly affect their behavior. One teacher, believing children must be molded, teaches loyalty to country by carefully censoring what students read and hear about democracy and communism. Another teacher, believing children learn best when confronted with all kinds of evidence, takes a different tack in teaching his class.

Teachers work in the midst of purposes: the nation's, the local community's, the administration's, the parents', the children's, and their own. Whether any of these ever achieve fulfillment will depend on the particular resolution the teacher makes in his own personal economy with respect to all these purposes. A major task of the teacher-education program must be to help the student explore these purposes and to arrive at his own understanding of them in so personal a way that they become a part of his very being.

Appropriate Methods of Teaching

As we have already suggested, the methods teachers use must fit the kinds of people they are. An effective teacher must have a stock of methods he may call upon as needed to carry out his teaching duties. These may vary widely from teacher to teacher and even from moment to moment. But whatever their nature they must fit the situations and purposes of the teacher and be appropriate for the students with whom they are used.

The teaching of methods has long been regarded as a prime function of teacher education. Indeed, there are some who have complained of a preoccupation with methods. The self-as-instrument concept of professional training, however, places a different emphasis on the matter. The teacher-education program must help each student find the methods best suited to him, to his purposes, his task, and the peculiar populations and problems with which he must deal on the job. This is not so much a matter of *teaching* methods as one of helping students to *discover* methods. It is a question of finding the methods right for the teacher rather than right for teaching.

In the chapters to follow we have tried to explore more

fully the implications of perceptual psychology for each of the five areas characteristic of effective professional workers.

ENDNOTES

[1]C. R. Rogers, "The Characteristics of a Helping Relationship," *Personnel and Guidance J.* 37 (1958): 6–16.

[2]A. W. Combs, D. L. Avila, W. W. Purkey, *Helping Relationships: Basic Concepts for the Helping Professions* (Boston: Allyn and Bacon, 1971).

[3]F. E. Fiedler, "The Concept of an Ideal Therapeutic Relationship," *J. Consult. Psych.* 14 (1950): 239–245.

[4]D. W. Soper and A. W. Combs, "The Helping Relationship as Seen by Teachers and Therapists," *J. Consult. Psych.* 26 (1962): 288.

[5]A. W. Combs and D. W. Soper, "The Helping Relationship as Described by 'Good' and 'Poor' Teachers," *J. Teacher Ed.* 14 (1963): 64–68.

[6]A. W. Combs and D. W. Soper, "Perceptual Organization of Effective Counselors," *J. Counsel. Psych.* 10, no. 3 (1963): 222–226.

[7]Margaret Lindsey, *New Horizons for the Teaching Profession* (Washington, D.C.: National Commission on Teacher Education and Professional Standards, N.E.A., 1961).

[8]W. W. Lynch, "Person Perception: Its Role in Teaching," *Indiana Univ. School of Ed. Bull.* 37 (1961): 1–37.

[9]A. W. Combs, "A Perceptual View of the Nature of 'Helpers' in Personality Theory and Counseling Practice," *Papers of Annual Conference on Personality Theory and Counseling Practice* (1961): 53–58

A. W. Combs, *Florida Studies in the Helping Professions* (Gainsville: University of Florida Press, 1969).

[10] A. W. Combs and D. W. Soper, "Perceptual Organization of Effective Counselors," *J. Counsel. Psych.* 10, no. 3 (1963): 222–226.

[11]John A. Benton, "Perceptual Characteristics of Episcopal Pastors," Unpublished Ed.D. Dissertation (Gainesville: University of Florida, 1964).

[12]C. T. Gooding, "An Observational Analysis of the Perceptual Organization of Effective Teachers," Unpublished Ed.D. Dissertation (Gainesville: University of Florida, 1964).

Robert S. Brown, "A Study of Perceptual Organization of Elementary and Secondary 'Outstanding Young Educators,' " Unpublished Doctoral Dissertation (Gainesville: University of Florida, 1970).

Herman G. Vonk, "The Relationship of Teacher Effectiveness to Perception of Self and Teaching Purposes," Unpublished Doctoral Dissertation (Gainesville: University of Florida, 1970).

D. A. Dellow, "A Study of the Perceptual Organization of Teachers and Conditions of Empathy, Congruence, and Positive Regard," Unpublished Doctoral Dissertation (Gainsville: University of Florida, 1971).

Charles Van Loan Dedrick, "The Relationship Between Perceptual Characteristics and Effective Teaching at the Junior College Level," Unpublished Doctoral Dissertation (Gainsville: University of Florida, 1972).

[13]Richard Usher and John Hanke, "The 'Third Force' in Psychology and College Teacher Effectiveness Research at the University of Northern Colorado," *Colorado Journal of Educational Research* 10, no. 2 (winter 1971).

[14]A. W. Combs and D. W. Soper, "Perceptual Organization of Effective Counselors," *J. Counsel. Psych.* 10, no. 3 (1963): 222–226.

[15]Benton, op. cit.

3

Creating Effective Teachers

Good teaching, we have suggested, is an intensely personal matter. It is a problem of personal discovery, of learning to use one's self as instrument. To achieve these ends prospective teachers must be provided more than a contemplation of subject matter and teaching techniques. The crucial test is in *doing* something with them.

CREATING EFFECTIVE PRACTITIONERS

For many years a misunderstanding has existed between those responsible for the subject-matter education of teachers and those responsible for the professional aspects of teacher preparation. This seems to have come about because of a confusion over purposes.

The purposes involved in producing a professional practitioner are different from those of producing a scholar. Where intentions are different, there must also be differing goals, techniques, and procedures for their realization. Failure to understand this fact is responsible for some of the friction and misunderstandings that arise between professors of education and their counterparts in the more traditional subject-matter areas.[1]

Everyone is familiar from his own behavior with the fact that there is a considerable gap between knowing and behaving. Most of us know a good deal better than we behave. Possessing knowledge is no guarantee that a person will use it. So, too, there is a difference between the scholar (knower) and practitioner (behaver). The education of the scholar is essentially directed toward content: the acquisition, organization, and understanding of information. The goal of the practitioner is the effective use of knowledge. For the scholar, content is crucial. For the practitioner, application is the heart of the task. It is possible for the scholar to learn his subject with little or no concern for action or for the human consequences of his understandings. The practitioner, on the other hand, primarily concerned about action and human welfare, may be able to practice on occasion with little concern for content. Both the scholar and the practitioner can, of course, exist in the same skin. When they do, that is marvelous. However, since we cannot keep people in school for unlimited periods of time, we usually have to be content with producing people who are more or less one or the other.

The responsibility of the teacher-education program is the development of professional workers, persons who can be counted on to act on knowledge as well as to have it. The dynamics involved in this difference between knowing and behaving are often not well enough understood.

Because the purposes of the scholar and practitioner are different, their values, goals, and methods of operation are likely to be different, too. As a consequence, communication between them often breaks down, and they pass each other like ships in the night. This kind of communication failure has often been responsible for the frictions occurring between subject-matter faculties and faculties in education. Such differences are by no means restricted to education, however. Scholars and practitioners in every discipline frequently fail to understand one another because they look through different glasses. This is true whether we are talking about the laboratory psychologist and the clinical psychologist, the biologist and the physician, the sociologist and the social worker, the physicist and the engineer, or the scholar and the teacher.

The ancient argument between scholar and practitioner will probably never be fully resolved. As long as people see what they do as important, they will probably continue to feel that what others do is less so. We can waste a good deal of time and energy getting embroiled in this kind of argument. We need to accept the fact that professional education *must* be different from content education, and this fact must be recognized by both faculty and students. In fact, if the day ever comes when the work going on in teachers' colleges is completely approved by those in colleges of arts and sciences then teacher-educators will know they have failed! They will have abrogated their essential purpose and betrayed their basic trust. Teacher-educators need to get on with the important business of producing the best practitioners possible to meet the pressing problems of our generation.

CREATING EFFECTIVE TEACHERS

Teacher education, like education generally, has done pretty well in two of its phases. It has been successful in gathering information and in making information available to students. We have done this by gathering information in our libraries and in the minds of brilliant teachers. We have learned also to make this information available to other people through lectures, demonstrations, and the whole new world of audio-visual techniques. We are experts at telling people what they need to know, and we measure the success of teaching by requiring students to tell it back to us. If they do this satisfactorily, we commend them for knowing and rest content that we have taught them well. Much of educational practice never gets beyond this level of learning. But there is a third phase of the learning process essential for teacher education, with which we have not done so well. It is helping people to discover the personal meaning of information so that they *behave* differently as a result of teaching. Research has shown that both good teachers and bad know what they ought to do. Most of us are like the old farmer who, when he was asked why he was not using modern methods, replied, "Heck, I ain't farmin' now half as well as I know how!"

THE PERCEPTUAL VIEW OF EFFECTIVE LEARNING

The perceptual psychologist views learning as a personal discovery of meaning by the student, a highly personal matter involving the way he sees himself and his experience. Let us take an example drawn from the first edition of this book to illustrate the point:

> At breakfast this morning I read in the paper about "pulmonic stenosis." Now I have told this to you. Any effect on your behavior? Probably not! This bit of information is very likely as strange to you as it was to me when I read it. It has little personal meaning and so affects your behavior very little. As isolated words whose meaning you do not know, this term has little effect. Now, suppose I tell you that this is a disorder of the heart and refers to a narrowing or closing of the pulmonary artery. The same piece of information now has a little more meaning for you. You may feel vaguely uncomfortable or hope that "This doesn't happen to me!" Let us go further. Suppose I tell you that this is a disorder with which some children are born and which, if not corrected, can have most serious consequences as a child grows older. If you are a teacher and concerned with children, the same piece of information is now a little closer. As a consequence it has more effect on your behavior. You pay more attention. You listen more intently. You think about it, speculate on it. Let us now give these words a little more personal meaning. Suppose you have just heard this phrase in a letter from the mother of one of the children in your class. She writes you that her child has pulmonary stenosis and will need to be operated on in the near future. The words now have a *much* more personal bearing and produce a number of effects on behavior. Perhaps you write to the

mother. You certainly discuss it with other teachers. You worry about it. You are especially nice to this child. Because this information has a more personal meaning for you, you behave much more precisely, much more certainly, with respect to it. Let us go one step further. Assume you have just been told by your doctor that you have this disorder yourself! Now, indeed, your behavior is deeply affected. All kinds of things may occur because of your new awareness!

The basic principle of learning in perceptual psychology is this: *Any item of information will affect an individual's behavior only in the degree to which he has discovered its personal meaning for him.*[2,3] The production of effective teachers will require helping each student to explore and discover his personal meanings about subject matter, people, purposes, and learning, and about methods and about himself. The source of many of our failures in teacher education, it now seems clear, is that we have not sufficiently understood that professional education must operate on these deeper, more personal, levels of learning. We have assumed that knowing and behaving are one and that the time-honored ways of teaching subject matter are appropriate for teaching people to teach as well. Our effort has been involved with teaching our students *about teaching* instead of helping them to *become teachers*. To the contrary, as we have seen, professional teacher education must be an intensely human process designed to involve the student deeply and personally.

THE CONDITIONS FOR EFFECTIVE LEARNING

To bring about the kind of learning we have been advocating for teacher education requires professional programs consciously and carefully designed to meet the three basic conditions for personal learning. These are as follows:

1. The creation of student needs for understanding.
2. The development of an atmosphere that makes the exploration of personal meaning possible.

3. Assistance and encouragement in the active exploration and discovery of personal meaning.

Creating Needs for Understanding

People do what they need to. This is a basic principle of behavior all of us have known for a long time. Yet, though we have known about it, we have not always effectively put it to work in teacher education. Sometimes we have not utilized it because, like many of our students, we know about it but have not yet discovered its personal meaning for us. Even when we have been aware of its importance, however, we may have failed to use it effectively for at least two reasons.

1. We have failed to see things from the learner's point of view. While it is true that people always do what they need to, it is not true that they do what an outsider feels they need to do. This difference in the perception of need has been a problem for generations. Teachers are intent upon what young people will need to know twenty years from now, while students are interested in finding out what they need to know right now.

Teachers and students live in different worlds. So it happens that the very knowledge possessed by the teacher may prevent him from perceiving the needs of his students. It is a difficult thing for the expert, having achieved a particular level of knowledge or experience, to set it aside and see things like a beginner.

2. A second difficulty in relating teacher education to need has to do with the goals we have in mind. Teacher-educators are often concerned with long-term goals, while the student is fundamentally motivated by short-term ones. Looking at what a student will need to know six months, a year, two years from now, we operate on the assumption that he, too, perceives such goals as meaningful. This seems logical enough, but unfortunately it does not work out in practice. The needs that have a maximum degree of effect on behavior are those needs the student perceives in the now. Though his

professor may be certain that an understanding of Dewey's philosophy will be helpful to the student as a teacher, the relationship between Dewey's philosophy and his immediate needs is by no means so clearly apparent to the student teacher. Since it is immediate needs that most strongly affect learning, we must utilize *current* needs of students.

Teacher education must do much more than understand and satisfy student needs, however. A program based solely on the satisfaction of present student needs would not get very far. The genius of good teaching is not simply the satisfaction of current needs but helping students search for new goals and objectives that they never had before.

One of the least effective ways to create needs is to tell students what is necessary to make them effective teachers. We have already seen that an emphasis on how teachers *ought* to behave is of limited help because it deals with symptoms, not with causes. The student who tries to behave in ways he does not understand or in ways unrelated to himself will find himself really frustrated.

The attempt to motivate young teachers by discussions in perceptual terms of what makes a teacher is only a little more rewarding because the previous experience of most students gets in the way of making this very effective. Most students have been so indoctrinated with the direct approach to behavioral change that the idea of seeking change through modification in their own beliefs and understandings often seems too complex and devious. It is hard to convince them that the time spent in looking, examining, exposing one's beliefs and ways of perceiving is not wasted. Because of their past experience, they have usually been thoroughly brainwashed into the belief that they are not learning anything unless they are being given more facts.

The most powerful needs, perceptual psychology tells us, are those which are seen as directly bearing on the self. Anyone who has ever had the experience of teaching beginning teachers on a college campus concurrently with experienced teachers in the field can attest to the importance of having real problems to find answers to. Questions that seem to be of vital concern to teachers in the field may seem to the student teacher on the campus as just another academic discussion. It is hard to get excited about artificial problems, but real ones, especially if they are one's own, have tremendous motivating power. This is not true of teaching alone. The importance of involvement in the training of professional workers is widely recognized in the other helping professions such as medicine, social work, nursing, psychology, and counseling.

Teacher-educators have long been convinced of the importance of involvement. This is, in part, the function of student teaching or the internship. Such involvement, however, is usually conceived as an opportunity to try what has already been learned, not as a means of creating the need to know. A full understanding of the importance of need in the control of learning calls for drastic revision of our conceptions of "student teaching" and "courses."

Historically, "practice teaching" has been perceived as a place where the student practiced what he had been taught in the teachers' college. So conceived, it seemed proper that it should come at the end of the student's program. If, however, active involvement in the classroom is to be understood, not only as a place for practicing solutions but, more importantly, a place for the *discovery of what the problems are*, then active involvement in schools should exist at every stage of the student's program from beginning to end. This value of involvement for the creation of needs to know is becoming widely recognized and many teachers' colleges are instituting programs of student involvement from the very first days of entrance into the professional sequence.

If the importance of need in learning is as vital as we have suggested above, change is also required in our traditional concept of college courses. Most college courses begin with the assumption that the student either has, or should have, a need to know the subject. Indeed, it is a rare college instructor who makes any significant attempt to relate his subject matter to the needs of the student and rarer still to find instructors who actively seek to *create* needs to know.

A typical college course is designed to present a student with an organized body of knowledge arranged in systematic fashion dictated by the nature of the subject matter or the need of the instructor. Unhappily students simply do not learn this way. Their needs for subject matter are rarely, if ever, systematic. Rather, their needs to know are very likely to appear to the scholarly professor so haphazard and fortuitous as to drive him to despair as he perceives the violence done his beautiful organized body of content.

Some teachers' colleges are currently breaking up traditional courses into smaller units sometimes known as "competencies," "learning modules," "mini teaching," "micro teaching," "precision teaching," "simulation," and the like. Providing instruction in smaller segments in this fashion certainly departs in promising fashion from the monolithic traditional course. Unhappily, such units are, more often than not, offered in prescribed sequence according to a preconceived plan rather than in response to student need and so suffer from the same basic weakness of the orthodox courses they replace. If the importance of need in learning is truly to be implemented in professional education, it seems clear better alternatives must be employed.

Developing an Atmosphere for Learning

Learning is a function of the individual's personal exploration and discovery of meaning. How likely this learning is to affect behavior of the individual will depend upon how important or close the idea is perceived in relation to the self. The personal discovery of meaning does not occur, however, where circumstances are threatening or where the self is regarded as intruder. Whether or not the exploration of meaning can occur will depend on the atmospheres we create.

When people feel threatened, two interesting things happen to their abilities to perceive. One of these is an effect which psychologists call "tunnel vision." The field of perception becomes narrowed down so that they perceive only the object that threatens them. This experience is familiar to all of us. We need but recall an instance when we have been seriously threatened to discover for ourselves how oblivious we became to the surrounding events in the midst of a threatening condition. "I couldn't think of a thing!" we say, or, "All I could see was that———!"

A second effect of threat is to make the individual defend his existing position. All of us are familiar with this dynamic too. Generally, the more threatened the individual becomes, the more steadfastly he defends his existing position. Now, clearly, these two effects of threat are antithetical to everything we are seeking in education. Surely we do not want students' perceptions to be narrowed. On the contrary, we want them to be opened up. Nor do we want individuals blindly to defend their existing positions; we want them to change their positions to something more effective. Since the individual's self is the most important and precious thing he owns, he is certainly not going to risk it in threatening situations. It follows, then, that in order to help an individual explore and discover personal meaning, we must begin by creating atmospheres sufficiently free of threat so that relationships to self can be explored and examined. Like a turtle, the self cannot go anywhere unless it sticks its neck out. But also like the turtle, the self will not venture forth from its shell unless it is safe enough out there to do so.

The elimination of threat from the learning situation does not mean that professors must coddle or shield prospective teachers. Quite the contrary, the task of teaching is to encourage and challenge students, to help them stretch themselves to their utmost. There is a difference between challenge and threat, however. Whether or not an individual feels challenged depends on whether he feels he is able to deal with the situation with which he is confronted. If he feels he is not able to deal with the situation before him, the feeling he has is one of threat rather than challenge, and the negative effects of threat we have described above are the consequence. The settings required for maximum professional growth are circumstances that challenge students but do not threaten them. To create this kind of atmosphere means that college instructors must be sensitive to the impact they have on student teachers for the distinction between threat and challenge lies not in what the teacher thinks he is doing but in what the students perceive him to be doing.

Basically, the atmosphere required for effective discovery of personal meaning is the same as that needed for the production of creativity, the expression of individuality. What restricts the individual's freedom to be and to express his deeper self makes him just that much less likely to be creative. Creativity is not learned from restraint. It calls for an atmosphere that encourages daring and venturing forth. Whatever narrows or hampers the exploration of ideas and their relationship to self must be rigorously eliminated from the teacher-education process. We need, rather, to find the very best means possible to create the kind of atmospheres that provide maximum freedom and openness.

Two chapters of the 1962 ASCD Yearbook are devoted to a discussion of ways in which teachers can encourage acceptance and openness to experience in children.[4] The suggestions are equally appropriate for adults hoping to be teachers themselves one day. The committee points out that conformity and creativity are antithetical—what produces one tends to destroy the other. The choice is clear. If we have conforming classrooms, we can be sure they will not be creative. If we want creative classrooms, we shall have to dispense with rigid controls, neatness, and externally imposed concepts of order. The atmosphere for self discovery is one that calls for teachers who are friendly representatives of society, there to assist the growing process by eliminating what hinders self-discovery while encouraging and aiding what makes discovery possible. The following are a few of the factors listed by the Yearbook committee as hindrances to creativity and the atmosphere for growth:

1. Preoccupation with order, categorization, and classifying.
2. Overvaluing authority, support, evidence, and the "scientific method"—all the good answers are someone else's.
3. Exclusive emphasis upon the historical view, implying that all the good things have been discovered already.
4. Cookbook approaches, filling in the blanks, etc.
5. Solitary learning, with its discouragement of communication.

6. The elimination of self from the classroom—only what the book says is important, not what I think.
7. Emphasis upon force, threat, or coercion. What diminishes the self diminishes creativity.
8. The idea that mistakes are sinful.
9. The idea that students are not to be trusted.
10. Lockstep organization.

On the other hand, the committee has suggested some of the following as factors producing atmospheres that encourage creativity:

1. The encouragement of fantasy and fun.
2. The provision of wide choices.
3. Trust in students so that they, in turn, can trust themselves.
4. Encouraging cooperative interaction.
5. Creating feelings of belonging.
6. Encouraging cooperation and discouraging competition.
7. Encouraging difference, uniqueness, and integrity.
8. Encouraging communication.
9. Encouraging problem-solving approaches.
10. Valuing openness and flexibility.
11. Valuing individuality.
12. Eliminating censorship.
13. Encouraging experimenting and trying.

The systematic examination of teacher-education practices in the light of these considerations might point the way to fruitful improvements in professional education.

Assisting the Discovery of Personal Meaning

Perceptual psychology has defined the basic principle of learning as the discovery of personal meaning. Whatever is done in teacher education must therefore be related to the student's self in important ways. For teacher-education faculties this calls for continuous awareness of the student's self and its conscious inclusion in every aspect of planning and operating programs. For the student, it calls for a high degree of self-direction and personal responsibility.

The important role of the self in teacher education may not be welcomed by some educators. For several generations we have treated scientific method and objectivity as sacred cows. For many, this has called for the rigorous exclusion of self from the classroom situation and heavy emphasis on "disciplined objectivity." In the experiments on effective helpers mentioned earlier, however, objectivity seems to correlate *negatively* with effectiveness! It seems clear that if the concept of learning advanced by modern perceptual psychology is accurate, the subjective experience of the individual must be admitted to the classroom.

In the old European universities the exploration and discovery of personal meaning was often accomplished in the interaction of students in the beer halls, which in those days were considered to be as vital a part of the university as the lecture hall. In this congenial setting students could get together to kick ideas around to their hearts' content. In comparison, many aspects of the modern American university seem almost perversely designed to prevent the kind of personal involvement required for effective learning. Huge classes, the discouragement of student cooperation, content orientation, objective testing, and the ever-lengthening infancy we impose on our young people de-emphasize the personal character of learning and discourage involvement of students in the learning process. The growth of interest in recent years in the utilization of discussion-group techniques seems at least one step in the right direction. We need many more.

This much seems certain: The personal exploration and discovery of meaning is not likely to occur unless it is valued by the faculty. To produce the kind of personal discovery of meaning about which we have been speaking, it will be necessary to place far less insistence on the weight of authority, proof, and external evidence while we encourage students to do their own looking, discovering, and thinking about professional problems. We will also need to encourage experimentation everywhere in the teacher-education program. This will not be easy for one of the characteristics of our profession is that it has been built on "right answers." Facts, correctness, authority, proof, "100 percent"—these have been the coin of the realm. To be wrong, to blunder, or to fail—these are things we have feared. Clearly, we cannot encourage experimentation and the personal discovery of meaning if making mistakes is practically synonymous with sinning. People learn from making mistakes, often more than from their successes. If we cannot permit mistakes, it should not surprise us if the product we turn out disappoints us with its conservatism and lack of imagination. People who are afraid to make mistakes will be afraid to try. People who do not try will surely not be creators or innovators.

Effective professional helpers are autonomous, self-directed, responsible persons. Responsibility, however, is not learned in a vacuum. Nobody ever learned to be responsible by having it withheld. People learn to be responsible from being *given* responsibility. It is learned like any other "subject," by success experience with increasingly larger and more difficult projects. A faculty, fearful that students may make mistakes, can seriously interfere with the development of responsibility. On the other hand, students coming to college after years of experience with authoritarian schools and teachers who discouraged independence take time to adjust to new ways of life and new expectations. Their first reactions to demands for self-direction and responsibility, therefore, are likely to be anxious and resistant. The solution for this dilemma requires of the faculty that self-direction and responsibility be honestly valued and encouraged and of the students that confronting the problems of becoming a teacher be seen as an exciting and constantly challenging test of personal growth and adequacy well worth the risks of getting involved.

The personal discovery of meaning calls for a program in which differences are valued and encouraged, in which wide choices are available, and in which personal decisions are met with respect and admiration. Prejudice and censorship can have no part in such a program. There must be freedom to look at and try almost anything. To produce this kind of situation will require the careful analysis of programs for the elimination of barriers that lie in the path of student exploration and the active encouragement of difference and choice. Both students and faculties must see education classrooms as laboratories for trying, erring, reworking, and trying again.

ENDNOTES

[1]G. K. Hodenfield and T. M. Stinnett, *The Education of Teachers* (Englewood Cliffs, N.J.: Prentice-Hall, 1961).

[2]A. W. Combs and O. Snygg, *Individual Behavior: A Perceptual Approach to Psychology* (New York: Harper & Row, 1959).

[3]A. W. Combs, D. Avila, and W. W. Purkey, *Helping Relationships: Basic Concepts for the Helping Professions* (Boston: Allyn & Bacon, 1971).

[4]A. W. Combs, ed., *Perceiving, Behaving, Becoming: A New Focus for Education*. 1962 ASCD Yearbook (Washington, D.C.: Association for Supervision and Curriculum Development, 1962).

4

The Good Teacher Is Well Informed

The first of the five characteristics attributed to the effective teacher in Chapter 2 was "a rich, extensive, and available field of perceptions about his subject." In other words, a good teacher must be well informed. This seems so obvious as to need no statement at all. Many critics of modern education, however, do not feel so.[1] Hearing teacher-educators talking much about the adjustment of the child, the process of learning, the philosophy and history of education, and so on, they become honestly concerned over what seems to them a de-emphasis of solid intellectual accomplishment in favor of such matters. The critics need have no fear, however; professional educators are keenly aware that teachers need to be well informed.

What seems like a lack of concern to the critic is actually an artifact of the way in which most teacher education in the United States is organized. Many teacher-education programs, particularly those in large universities, have little, if any, control over the subject-matter preparation of their students. This portion of teacher education is the responsibility of the traditional academic departments in the university. As Charles Silberman points out in his *Crisis in the Classroom*, the academic departments are responsible for two-thirds to three-fourths of most prospective teachers' formal programs.[2]

Typically, the student teachers' experience with subject matter is acquired from academic scholars, while the professional educator is assigned the responsibility for the how and why of teaching. What seems like a lack of concern for subject matter is often a mere product of the division of labor. People naturally talk most about the things for which they are responsible.

The purpose of this book is to explore the professional aspects of teacher education. The content preparation of teachers is a subject for several other books. However, the successful professional school cannot ignore the student's subject-matter experiences even if it has no direct control over them. The student's experience with his teachers in the content areas provides him with a live demonstration of his subject being taught. The subject-matter professor is teaching the *way to teach* as well as *what to teach*, even though this may not be his intention at all. What students learn as a consequence of this experience is often much more lasting than that about which they are only told. There is a saying among teacher-educators that "Teachers teach the way they have been taught rather than the way we taught them to teach." Students do not enter teacher-preparation programs without experience in teaching. They enter with twelve to fifteen years of having been taught.

Professional education must spend much time helping students see that there are other ways of teaching than those they may have been exposed to thus far. Often this is not easy. It is difficult for students to learn to discount their past experiences. Nor is it easy to persuade professors to change their ways of teaching. There is nothing more sacrosanct on a college campus than academic freedom, which often may be interpreted to mean the professor's inalienable right to teach excruciatingly badly! The subject-matter preparation of teachers cannot be ignored, however, and the educator must continually use his influence to improve the quality of subject-matter teaching wherever and whenever possible. In the remainder of this chapter let us examine some of the more outstanding factors that seem related to the subject-matter preparation of teachers.

THE SELECTION OF CONTENT

Some Factors in Content Selection

Teachers need to be well informed. But about what? Once it was easy to answer that question, but the answers are no longer simple. Three current factors that make it difficult to determine what teachers need to know are the information explosion, changing social needs, and changing concepts of what information is pertinent.

The Information Explosion. The amount of information available to human beings today is so much greater than that possessed by our forebears as to stagger the imagination. There was a time when comparatively few subjects, once mastered, could guarantee that a man might live for the rest of his days revered as a scholar and a wise man by his fellows. But those days are gone forever! The facts known to man have proliferated at such speed that a scholar today can count himself lucky if he is able to encompass in a lifetime all that is known even in a very limited field of knowledge.

To be well informed in these times is a different thing than it was fifty, or even twenty, years ago. The old concepts of what is essential are no longer valid. The information explosion has made it impossible ever again to define a curriculum as a set body of information to be required of everyone. There is only a vast body of tentative facts from which to make choices.

The Changing Needs of Society. The proper selection of content for teachers is further complicated by the increasing variety of human needs. Adam Smith wrote, in 1776, that man's needs were for food, shelter, and clothing. Even in those days, however, such a definition of human need was only partly true. In the replete societies of today, it is totally inadequate.

The extent of modern man's needs seems almost limitless. The schooling needed for the wealthy dilettante of generations ago is a far cry from the needs of the modern citizen with a job to do and responsibilities to meet in a more and more complicated world. When choices were limited, we could be sure about what was good to know. With the choices open to us today who shall say with certainty what any man *must* know?

This much is certain: The narrow curriculum suitable a hundred years ago is as out of date now as the horse and buggy. We expect our schools to provide us with a vast army of persons able to assume the duties and carry out the functions of a tremendously complex technological existence. No single curriculum can provide us with such diversity. A variety of teachers with many different skills are called for.

Changing Concepts of Teacher Needs for Information. What the teacher needs to know will depend on this particular professional task. The good teacher needs all the information he can get, but not all information is of equal importance for him. What information is required will depend on the level he is expected to teach, the nature and backgrounds of his students, the equipment available, the needs of students and community, and a hundred other factors. The kind and depth of content required for the primary, elementary, junior high, senior high, and junior college teacher varies greatly depending upon the particular responsibilities the well-informed teacher must carry out.[3]

It is apparent that the concept of the teacher as wise man and fountainhead of information is long outmoded. Once we could expect that most of the facts required by his students would be at the teacher's fingertips. But where could one find such a teacher today? A kindergarten teacher, accustomed to thinking of herself as fairly well informed, recently reported with some shock the amused toleration of her class as they set her straight on space terminology! Today's teacher will often be working with students far better informed than he in dozens of areas, sometimes even in the very area the teacher is trying to teach!

As Alvin Toffler reminds us in *Future Shock*, our culture is evolving at a dizzy pace.[4] In our quest for certainty and security it is increasingly difficult to anchor ourselves to packets of "essential" information and clusters of "right" values. This does not mean that we need despair or permit ourselves to be swept helplessly along by uncontrollable forces. What *is* called for is the cultivation of attitudes and beliefs that will equip us to cope adequately with and give responsible direction to our ever-changing culture. For the educator this requires an ability to inspire student development of thought processes that are socially sensitive, critically reflective, adaptable, and global in scope. For this we need sensitive, imaginative, resourceful—and, at times, audacious—teachers. Clearly the preparation process for this type of teacher cannot be moored to "learning" experiences that are dominated by the ingestion-regurgitation of "essential" facts.

Even if we could hope to produce a teacher with the "right" information for today's world it would almost certainly not be right for tomorrow's. Education is one of the few industries to turn out its product twenty years *after* the demand. Since we cannot foresee the future with certainty, we cannot hope to teach today all that people must know tomorrow. Our only salvation is the production of intelligent people. For that we need intelligent teachers, *knowing* persons. This "knowing" may be general or highly specific. Either way, teacher education must produce intelligent, informed human beings. Mere storehouses of information are not enough.

It is always a temptation in looking for answers to educational problems to seek across-the-board solutions that can be applied in all times and in all places. This usually turns out to be a pipe dream. Such solutions simply do not exist. The same content demands cannot be made of all students in training for the profession. We cannot expect a kindergarten or first-grade teacher to have the specialized knowledge of the instructor in astronomy at the college level. Nor can we demand of the high school teacher that he have at his instant command the ingenious array of information and techniques required of the busy kindergarten teacher. What is needed is both a broad general education designed for the development of intelligent, effective citizens and a program of specialization aimed at preparing the teacher for the particular professional task he will later be expected to fill.

The General Education Program

The making of a teacher begins with an intelligent layman. For the preparation of teachers we need the best general education program we are able to devise.[5] Such a program does not need to be specially devised for teachers. Neither should it be a watered-down affair taught with disdain for people who are not going to major in their subject. Teachers need the same high quality program in general education that we seek for all beginning college students. Indeed, because they are going to be teachers, this is more important for them than for anyone.

Unhappily the level of teaching in general education programs in many of our colleges leaves much to be desired. Overwhelmed with students and charged with the responsibility for "weeding them out," harassed instructors often cover the subject as best they can and escape as quickly as possible to teaching the "majors." As a consequence, general education programs are often badly taught and deadly dull. This is not good for any student. For education students it is disastrous.

Content Specialization

In addition to his general education preparation, the student teacher needs one or more areas of specialization in the particular content that he will be responsible for teaching. This is usually acquired by selecting courses from those offered by the various subject-matter departments of the college or university. Many provide very rich and rewarding opportunities for learning. For students expecting to teach specific subjects in high school or junior college, this kind of course organization presents no great problem. For the student planning to teach in an area cutting across subject-matter lines, however, or for the teacher preparing to work in the elementary grades, it is another matter. Their subject-matter needs often do not fit the traditional college pattern.[6]

The elementary teacher has a specialty. It is teaching general education. For this he needs preparation in breadth over a number of subjects rather than depth in one or two, but few colleges are organized to provide this for him. Courses in the various subject-matter departments are generally designed with majors in mind and tend to become increasingly specialized, so that the student who should spread his attention over a number of areas can seldom acquire the kind of experience he needs.

In some colleges the failure to understand the task of the elementary teacher has created morale problems as well. It has sometimes happened, for example, that elementary teachers have been accused of ignorance and treated as second-class citizens by professors who have equated depth of knowledge with scholarship. This is most unfair. The elementary teacher's specialization in general education is legitimate and necessary. It is a different order of specialization but surely not a less important one! The content required for general education is not less, only broader.

ACQUIRING CONTENT

Making Content Meaningful

Content must be meaningful; it is not an end in itself. It is not enough to produce teachers who *collect facts.* We must find ways of producing teachers who *find meaning in facts* and who help their students to do so. There are limits to what any teacher can or should know. Whether we like it or not, we shall often have to be content with having our children taught by teachers who do not know all about the subject. The good teacher's task is to stimulate and facilitate learning. The measure of his success is not the degree to which his students are like him, but the degree to which he has assisted his students to transcend him.

Facts are no more than tools for the solution of problems. There are no facts which a person must know except in the light of his purposes and goals. As Johnson and Swan have expressed it,

> The simple addition of more and more facts does not produce better and better education. If this were true, teaching children would be a pretty simple and straightforward proposition. We could simply add more of everything: more time in the school years, more hours in the school day, more pages in books, more facts for the memory. It is possible though that we have already reached the saturation level from the standpoint of "more" and we may be justified in viewing with alarm the degree to which we sacrifice reasoning and thinking on the altar of content. Perhaps it is equally true that we substitute presenting facts to our students for presenting seasoned and matured thinking of our own. The simple recitation of facts and the demanding of their recall on schedule is an effective way to dodge the issue of thinking for ourselves and for suggesting challenging ideas. It is disquieting to consider this: if our recital of facts were stripped from us would we stand intellectually naked in front of the class?[7]

It is only as the meaning of facts is perceived that they become useful and effective tools for the advancement of human understanding and happiness. It is this concern for meaning that has caused many teachers to be increasingly concerned with the *structure* of content rather than the collection and dissemination of facts. Bruner has expressed the matter in this way:

> Mastery of the fundamental ideas of a field involves not only the grasping of general principles, but also the development of an attitude toward learning and inquiry, toward guessing and hunches, toward the possibility of

> solving problems on one's own. Just as a physicist has certain attitudes about the ultimate orderliness of nature and a conviction that order can be discovered, so a young physics student needs some working version of these attitudes if he is to organize his learning in such a way as to make what he learns useable and meaningful in his thinking. To instill such attitudes by teaching requires something more than the mere presentation of fundamental ideas. Just what it takes to bring off such teaching is something on which a great deal of research is needed, but it would seem that an important ingredient is a sense of excitement about discovery—discovery of regularities of previously unrecognized relations and similarities between ideas, with a resulting sense of self-confidence in one's abilities.[8]

The current concern for the structure of content seems like an important step forward. Its value, however, may be subverted if it is seen as no more than an emphasis on principles rather than details in the teaching of content. Meaning is not a function of the organization of subject matter. It is not something given to the student but something the student discovers for himself. He does not acquire it from outside, he finds it within himself. The discovery of meaning is a personal process involving the student's own purposes, values, goals, concepts, and needs. The organization of content and the emphases of the instructor can help in the process of discovering meaning. It is no guarantee that the discovery will occur.

Unhappily the discovery of meaning by students is often badly impeded in many college classrooms by an emphasis on trifling detail. Concepts and generalizations in any subject are comparatively few, but details are myriad. An instructor talking about generalizations would quickly run out of material, but he can talk about details forever! Small wonder that students "get the message" that the instructor believes details are the important things.

Detail by itself is meaningless. Unless detail is placed in an overall pattern it is rapidly forgotten. One needs but to watch a group of college students preparing for examinations to understand how thoroughly they have been impressed with the importance of detail. They know that good grades depend not on one's grasp of generalizations, but on one's ability to demonstrate knowledge of details. To make matters worse, we are committed to a grading system that requires the distribution of students along a continuum. The more they can be spread out, the easier it is to assign and justify grades. But with better and better students coming to college as a consequence of tighter requirements for selection the only way in which such a spread can be produced is through testing students more and more intensively on the nonessentials. So we are forced by the demands of our examination and grading system to be preoccupied with details at the expense of meaning. Teacher education must combat this creeping paralysis whenever it occurs, both inside and outside its immediate area of responsibility. What good is a teacher who knows facts but not what they mean?

In recent years we have come to see the process of learning as an emerging process. We now understand it as a matter of exploring and discovering on the part of the student rather than a process of injection on the part of the teacher. This shift in our thinking has paid vast dividends everywhere in public education. This does not mean that an organized, systematic consideration of subject matter is *per se* antithetical to student-centered teaching. It is possible for a teacher to be deeply student-centered in his approach to teaching, while at the same time his work is organized around a systematized body of subject matter. The problem is not to be stated as either/or; it is rather, What is the place of organized approaches to subject matter in student-centered learning? Since the codification and organization of principles can only follow the acquisition of facts and principles, the beginner in any discipline must be much less concerned with the organization of knowledge than he will be at later stages in his development. As Bode expressed it, the student must begin with a *psychological order* of subject matter and end with a *logical order.*[9] At later stages of a given topic the student himself will find a need for his subject matter to be organized into a system.

Relating Content to Student Purposes

Instructors who work with education students must be aware that the purposes of such students may be different from liberal arts students in the very same classes. It is a basic principle of learning that whatever is learned is a function of the purposes of the learner. It follows, therefore, that whatever is taught in subject-matter classes needs to be closely related to the purposes of the students. In their enthusiasm for their subject, professors often find it hard to believe that others do not find their topic as fascinating and exciting as they do. Subject matter is, therefore, often taught as though all students were committed to devoting their lives to the study of that subject. Some of them may. But the person preparing to teach usually has no intention of doing deep research in the subject. If he is a grade school teacher, he may even be interested in the subject only as it contributes to his general background. Even students who are preparing to teach at the secondary level may have chosen the teaching profession because they are interested in working with young people and so regard subject matter as the *vehicle* they use to teach rather than something to be learned for its own sake.

Teachers are practitioners. Their concern is with the dissemination, application, and use of information. It is to be hoped they might be scholars too, but not in the same sense as one would expect of the student preparing to spend his life in research. This view of the uses of subject matter often lands the education student right in the middle of the practitioner-scholar controversy. In all innocence he may find himself sitting in classes surrounded by students who see themselves as scholars, experts, and scientists and who hold education students in contempt. He may even be as unlucky as to find that the professor himself subscribes to such attitudes. Although the neophyte teacher's purposes are different, they are not unimportant. We cannot afford to produce teachers who see themselves as second-rate and who must apologize for being what they are. Nor can we afford to produce teachers whose own experience with subject matter has brought them to the conclusion that the way to get subject matter across is through the humiliation and embarrassment of students.

Communicating Effectively

The student's grasp of content will be determined in large measure by the success of the instructor in communicating it. Communication, regarded by some instructors as an automatic concomitant of presenting the subject matter, is much more than this; it is a skill to be learned in its own right, and it has not occurred until something happens in the learner.

It is a common complaint of professors that students do not hear or understand what they are trying to tell them. The usual assumption is that the student is not meeting his responsibility. For example, a college professor might complain that it is *necessary to fail over 50 percent of his class.* To him this is a clear indication that modern students are stupid and/or lazy. This, in spite of the fact that college students today are more highly selected than ever before in history! The question might well be raised: Who has failed—the student or the teacher?

The primary responsibility for communication is always with the communicator, not the listener, and the teacher need not sacrifice scholarship to be understood. Einstein enjoyed talking to adolescents, and many of our most famous scientists have been able to communicate effectively with congressional committees.

Another factor interfering with effective communication is the widespread belief that students should be introduced to subject matter in such a fashion that all possible points of view are presented. It seems logical that the way to produce an open-minded, well-informed scholar is to confront him with all the possible data and let him arrive at his own best conclusions. Unfortunately, people do not learn logically. Learning is a question of meaning, and meaning is a matter of discovering the interrelationships of things. Discovery may actually be impeded by too great a flood of data. There is a world of difference between the situation experienced by the learned scholar critically looking at many points of view from the security of his established position and that of the beginner asked to cope with a bewildering flood of ideas without such security. Knowing a subject and knowing about it are by no means the same. Communication is not just a matter of presenting data. It is a function of discovery and development of meanings.

Involving the Student in the Subject Matter

No matter how well subject matter is presented, it will have no effect on the student until he has become personally involved in the learning process. Learning is not passive. It is an active process, requiring a personal commitment on the part of the learner. A great deal of college teaching violates this principle.

The impersonality of much of our teaching was bad enough in years past. With television and teaching machines we now seek to teach students by the hundreds without the teacher present at all! There is no doubt that a kind of rote learning, sufficient to pass examinations, can often be experienced by students under these circumstances. It is not enough for prospective teachers. The student who is going to teach must have a much deeper, more meaningful grasp of content than this.

The terrible competition for grades, which has become a normal part of college curricula, has a negative effect on developing student commitment. Grades limit and inhibit learning. The kind of knowing required for getting A's seldom leaves room for the student's own purposes or involvement. It is guessing what the instructor thinks is important and parroting it back to him with efficiency that pays off. Students quickly learn to set aside their own interests and to spend their energies in memorization rather than understanding.

One way to assist the aspiring teacher to discover meaning for what he learns in the classroom is to participate in the field experiences that illustrate abstract learnings. Unfortunately, this often means a one-semester trial run "student teaching" experience. An infinitely more effective approach is to become involved in ongoing field experiences that span the entire professional program. As the authors of this book can heartily attest, under such conditions substantive learnings take on life and color when the future teacher is enabled to see that Ivy Hall does relate meaningfully to P.S. 180. For example, a prospective teacher enrolled in a Social Foundations of Education course can read *about,* write *about,* recite *about* the self-fulfilling prophecy that frequently victimizes minority group youngsters. The concept takes on personal meaning, however, as the teacher-to-be witnesses the "we can't expect too much from them" syndrome actually occurring in real school and community settings. Meaningful learning involves *seeing* and *feeling* experiences, not merely *looking* at them.

Many of our most hallowed college traditions seem expressly designed to prevent the kind of involvement we now know is essential to effective learning. So much effort is expended in teaching the student what is already known that little time or opportunity remains to enable him to discover what he can for himself. The scholar certainly needs to know and respect the work of his forebears, but this can be carried too far. The student who learns that all the good answers, all the right answers, all the approved answers lie "out there" in what others have done or said or thought may end by becoming apathetic or discouraged at the possibilities of his own contributions. In a world needing creative people as much as ours, this is a wasteful, even dangerous, occurrence. In order to become effective teachers, teachers-in-training need to *experience* subject matter, to wade around in it, to make mistakes in it, to be intensely and personally in interaction with it, till it becomes a part of their very being. They must feel they are participants in it and contributors to it.

The Need for Inspired Instruction

It is essential that young people setting out to become teachers experience a sense of the wonder as well as the toil of learning a subject. To acquire this they need contact with the most inspiring and enthusiastic instructors available in the subject-matter areas. But often such instructors are available only in specialized courses taken by subject-matter majors, or their time is much occupied with research or administrative duties. This is a great pity. All our students, particularly those preparing for the teaching profession, need as much inspired instruction as can possibly be provided for them.

We cannot afford to turn out dull and pedantic teachers for these discourage students and subvert the purposes of education. A necessary requirement for good teaching is the capacity to fire the imagination. It is the satisfaction of search and discovery that motivates learning and provides new knowledge. If we are to produce teachers capable of such inspired teaching, we must select the most inspired teachers for them. It is a curious thing that our deep reverence for the scientific method often expresses itself in the dullest of teaching. Many instructors try so hard to be "detached" that they end up "out of touch." But to care about one's subject is not unscientific, and the rigor and respect for his subject demanded of the scientist are not incompatible with excitement and enthusiasm.

Understanding the Nature of Learning

Since teacher-education students learn from their own experience not only subject matter but also how to teach it, teacher-preparation programs cannot afford to overlook this aspect of teacher training. They must be concerned about the quality of subject-matter teaching wherever their students learn it and must do much more to disseminate what is known about the process of learning among their colleagues elsewhere in the college or university. There is a gulf between the best we know about learning and its implementation in practice. It is imperative that this lag between knowledge and practice be reduced as quickly as possible—not only for teacher-education students but for all college students. Ways must be found to introduce into the thinking of teachers at every level the very best concepts of the nature of learning that we possess.

Wider understanding of the learning process might go far toward reducing some of the most destructive criticism currently leveled at teachers and the programs they come from. Many of the things done in teachers' colleges are attempts to put into operation modern concepts about the process of learning. To persons outside education who conceive of learning as a simple process of telling and listening, these things may seem unrelated to the job to be done.

It is often assumed that learning is a simple process of presentation and absorption. Learning is rarely seen as a process to be investigated by scientific methods. Like many other human interrelationships it is lived with, dealt with daily, but seldom regarded as a matter to be studied or subjected to the scientific procedures that have carried us so far in other spheres of life. Learning *is* subject to scrutiny and there *are* things we know about it. Teacher-education curricula are based on the assumption that learning is a lawful, predictable, teachable function. This is their reason for being.

The knowledge we have about learning has been acquired in the same painstaking, carefully controlled kind of experimentation that has made possible the great advances of the other sciences. It is composed of facts and principles about an important human process, and it deserves the same respect and understanding as any other body of scientific knowledge. Once it was the senior author's privilege to work as a consultant with the faculty of a college of agriculture who were interested in improving the teaching methods used in their college. He spoke to them of the things we know that affect the efficiency of learning. Among these were such things as the relationship of learning to student motivation, needs, readiness, perception, meaning, and emotional condition on the one hand, and the atmosphere and conditions of learning on the other, including such matters as the role of the teacher, the principles of effective communication, the effects of threat and coercion, and the utilization of various sense modalities in learning. During the discussion that followed a professor of agronomy complained about this complexity. "Mr. Combs," he said, "all this may be very well for you as an educational psychologist, but it has nothing to do with the teaching of agronomy. I do not have time to be concerned about such things. I have all I can do just to get my subject across!" This same professor, because of his careful study of soils, knows that in order to grow a plant well it is necessary to deal with all the conditions affecting growth—amount of moisture, proper balance of acidity and alkalinity, and so on. He would not think of telling the farmer to forget these conditions any more than he would say, "I know my car needs a carburetor to run, but I'm going to run mine without one!" Yet in his own teaching he does exactly that. The principles of learning can no more be suspended than any other scientifically derived understanding. They continue to operate whether we are aware of them or not. If we ignore them, we do so at the risk of making teaching haphazard and ineffective.

Preparation As a Never-Ending Process

Many young people entering teaching seem to have the nction that preparation for teaching a subject is completed on graduation from college. They have an idea that Shakespeare, algebra, or dress design is a kind of unit, capable of completion, instead of an ongoing, never-ending area for search and discovery. College courses may often be but a minor part of professional preparation. No course or program of courses can ever hope to provide the teacher with all the answers to all the problems he will confront in the course of his teaching experience. Nor should they try to.

In recent years we have had some beautiful examples of misconceptions about subject matter brought home to us. We have awakened to discover that many of our teachers are woefully behind the current position of knowledge in their fields, especially in the fields of mathematics and science. New discovery moves at such a pace in almost every field of study that it does not take long to fall out-of-date even with the best of undergraduate preparation. Like *Alice in Wonderland* one must run as fast as one can just to stay where one is.

Effective preparation in subject matter is not just a question of the accumulation of credits. It is the development of an attitude of continual research and discovery. For the teacher, as for all professional practitioners, this implies being aware of and sensitive to the sources on which he might draw in seeking to enrich his professional activities: students; colleagues; the better professional literature; and, most crucially, the ever-experiencing self. Teachers are not merely disseminators of subject matter, they are participants in it. The training of teachers in subject matter must instill in them a problem-solving approach to their subject and a need for never-ending preparation. Teacher-training curricula must exert every influence to see that students are exposed to such approaches to subject matter.

ENDNOTES

[1]J. D. Koerner, *The Miseducation of American Teachers* (Boston: Houghton Mifflin, 1963).

[2]Charles Silberman, *Crisis in the Classroom* (New York: Random House, 1970), p. 377.

[3]G. W. Denmark, ed., *Criteria for Curriculum Decisions in Teacher Education* (Washington, D.C.: Association for Supervision and Curriculum Development, 1964).

[4]Alvin Toffler, *Future Shock* (New York: Random House, 1970).

[5]Margaret Lindsey, *New Horizons for the Teaching Profession* (Washington, D.C.: National Commission on Teacher Education and Professional Standards, N.E.A., 1961).

[6]G. K. Hodenfield and T. M. Stinnett, *The Education of Teachers* (Englewood Cliffs, N.J.: Prentice-Hall, 1961).

[7]V. B. Johnson and Beverly Swan, "Cult of Content," *Ed. Leadership* 19 (1961): 118–121.

[8]J. S. Bruner, *The Process of Education* (New York: Vintage Books, 1963).

[9]Boyd Henry Bode, *How We Learn* (Boston: D.C. Heath, 1940). pp. 146–147.

5

The Teacher's Beliefs about People

The professional preparation of teachers must begin with the student's beliefs about what people are like and why they behave as they do. A prime requisite for good teaching is the clearest, most useful understanding of the nature of people and their behavior existing in our generation because teachers, like everyone else, behave in terms of what seems to them to be so. A false or inaccurate conception of what his students are like provides the teacher with an inadequate basis for making decisions and guiding the learning process. Only when the teacher's perceptions about student behavior are accurate and available when he needs them can we be sure his attempts to teach will be effective.

THE EFFECTIVE TEACHER'S CONCEPTS ABOUT PEOPLE

What kinds of beliefs about people are characteristic of effective professional workers? A series of researches at the

University of Florida and the University of Northern Colorado investigated the perceptual differences between good and poor professional workers in teaching,[1,2,3,4,5,6,7] counseling,[2] nursing,[2] and the ministry.[2] Applying the findings of these studies to education it appears that good teachers can be clearly distinguished from poor ones with respect to the following beliefs about people:

Able-Unable. The good teacher perceives others as having the capacities to deal with their problems successfully. He believes that they can find adequate solutions to events, as opposed to doubting the capacity of people to handle themselves and their lives.

Friendly-Unfriendly. The good teacher sees others as being friendly and enhancing. He does not regard them as threatening to himself but rather sees them as essentially well-intentioned rather than evil-intentioned.

Worthy-Unworthy. The good teacher tends to see other people as being worthy rather than unworthy. He sees them as possessing a dignity and integrity that must be respected and maintained rather than seeing them as unimportant, as people whose integrity may be violated or treated as of little account.

Internally-Externally Motivated. The good teacher sees people and their behavior as essentially developing from within rather than as a product of external events to be molded and manipulated; he sees people as creative and dynamic rather than passive or inert.

Dependable-Undependable. The good teacher sees people as essentially trustworthy and dependable in the sense of behaving in a lawful way. He regards their behavior as understandable rather than capricious, unpredictable, or negative.

Helpful-Hindering. The good teacher sees people as being potentially fulfilling and enhancing to self rather than impeding or threatening. He regards people as important sources of satisfaction rather than sources of frustration and suspicion.

No doubt other research studies will add to this list in time. Meanwhile, the factors described in these studies provide us with guideposts to action. They describe some of the kinds of beliefs about people that students need to acquire in the course of training and suggest some factors in the kinds of programs we need in order to bring such perceptions into being.

HELPING STUDENTS FORMULATE ADEQUATE CONCEPTS ABOUT PEOPLE

Since perceptions are acquired from experience, students may develop adequate beliefs about people by exposure to new ideas and concepts: from established bodies of knowledge, through personal experience, in interaction with the beliefs of teachers, and through personal involvement with children and adults. But even such experience is not enough until the student has discovered the *meaning* of this experience and incorporated it into his own belief system.

The Contribution of Traditional Psychology

The need for understanding about people and behavior is widely recognized and has long been a part of the curriculum. Almost every teacher-education curriculum includes such courses as Human Growth and Development, the Psychology of Childhood, the Psychology of Adolescence, Educational Psychology, or similar courses designed to acquaint the teacher-in-training with the best that is known about human behavior.

For the most part these approaches to understanding behavior have been based on the stimulus-response frame of reference characteristic of American psychology since 1920. This concept seeks the causes of behavior in the forces at work on the individual from his heredity, his physiological condition, and/or his environment. Its basic tenet is that the behavior of people is the product of the forces to which they have been subjected in the process of growing up. It is essentially a descriptive, diagnostic view of behavior.

This view of behavior marked a great step forward for the social sciences when it first appeared, and it has provided the basis for many of the important contributions of those disciplines. It has also had a tremendous influence throughout our society generally. Its concepts are on everyone's tongue, and its principles are applied more or less successfully everywhere. In education it has been valuable in providing a frame of reference for attacking many problems of the profession. For thousands of teachers, for example, it has provided a background against which the behavior of children could be more adequately diagnosed. For administrators and supervisors it has provided essential data for curriculum revision and program planning.

Despite its contributions, however, stimulus-response psychology has three serious inadequacies which prevent it from making the larger contributions educators need: (1) It is essentially mechanistic rather than personalistic. That is to say, it provides us with important information about what *people in general* are like or what *people in general* may do but ignores what goes on inside a particular person when he behaves as he does. (2) It is diagnostically rather than treatment-oriented. It tells us, often very effectively, how people get like this or what forces caused a given behavior to occur but adds very little to helping us know what needs to be done about the matter. (3) It is inconsistent with modern educational philosophy. Traditional psychology is essentially mechanistic and manipulative whereas modern educational philosophy calls for a growth or facilitating approach to teaching.

The traditional approach to psychology prides itself on being "hard-nosed," on studying people objectively, scientifically, and dispassionately. This has been fruitful in providing us with much important information about human behavior. But the kinds of beliefs about people described in the research mentioned above are not acquired from information alone.

Knowledge of facts about behavior may contribute to the development of beliefs, but it cannot be counted on to produce them single-handedly.

The Contributions of Perceptual Psychology

In recent years the inclusion of perceptual approaches to psychology in teacher-education programs has provided many teachers with a second pair of glasses through which to look at behavior. Perceptual psychology is a personal, dynamic, treatment-oriented view of behavior developed largely by clinical psychologists, whose problem, like that of the teacher, is understanding the behavior of individuals. It is a psychology directly concerned with human perceptions, beliefs, and values, and many teacher-preparation programs have already incorporated this frame of reference into their curricula. It fits so well the needs of educators as to seem almost tailor-made for the teaching profession.

We have already pointed out in Chapter 2 how perceptual psychology emphasizes the personal qualities of human experience. It seeks the causes of behavior in meanings. It is also more directly action-oriented. Teachers need a psychology that makes it possible to deal with children in the present—in the here-and-now, face-to-face relationship of the classroom. It must offer clues about *people* who learn, as well as the *process* of learning. Perceptual psychology does this.

It assures the teacher that he can be a helpful force even in the life of the most difficult child. If behavior is a function of perception, then, if we can understand how the child is perceiving in the present, there are things we can do right now to help him grow and develop—even if we know nothing whatever about his past or his family life!

A point of view about human behavior that demands the manipulation and control of the individual's environment in order to help him has serious limitations for treatment. The older the child gets, the larger and larger the world to which he is responding becomes, and the less we have a chance of controlling and redirecting that world. It is a simple thing to remove harmful medicine from the neighborhood of a baby. The problems involved in removing drugs or alcohol from the environment of a teen-ager or a full-grown adult, however, are a different matter! The older the individual, the more we must depend on producing a change in his personal world rather than in the outer world in which he happens to be moving. This calls for changes in how he is seeing and believing and feeling about things. It also calls for sensitivity and understanding in those who would help him. One must acquire the ability to feel and perceive as another does. The preparation of such empathic teachers requires a perceptual psychology.

The value of the perceptual view of behavior is by no means restricted to mental hygiene problems. Learning itself is a matter of perceiving. Unless a child perceives differently, he has not learned at all. It is the goal of education to produce citizens capable of perceiving more broadly, more accurately, and more richly. This calls for teachers who are keenly aware of the perceputal world of their students and who can as a result facilitate the processes of learning. Understanding arithmetic, literature, physical education, or geography is a question of perceiving, and the teacher equipped with a perceptual view of behavior will be more adequately prepared to help children grow intellectually as well as emotionally. Individual, perceptual, or personalistic psychology is consistent with the democratic belief that when men are free to explore and discover they can find their own best ways. It is also consistent with modern educational beliefs and practices.

To many teachers the perceptual view of behavior comes as a refreshing breeze. It means that what they do is always important. Teachers and children are not merely victims of circumstance; there are things they can do to control their destinies and guide their fates. It is a fascinating and heart-warming experience to watch the excitement of experienced teachers exposed to perceptual views of behavior for the first time. It speaks to them in language they understand and provides practical answers to knotty problems that have harried them for years. They find in it a new tool especially suited to their tasks.

The six characteristics of good teachers reported in the research at the beginning of this chapter are all ways of looking at people in the very manner suggested by perceptual psychology. Most of the teachers in these experiments had never heard of perceptual psychology, yet they had somehow learned to look at their students in this fashion. Apparently, good teachers arrive at this frame of reference with respect to people as a consequence of their experience. Helping education students learn to look at behavior from the perceptual viewpoint is usually not a difficult matter. They pick it up naturally and easily. It fits their experience so smoothly they think they have always known it!

Since perceptual psychology provides a frame of reference that is so well suited to the profession of teaching it is time we introduced it much more widely to our teacher-training programs. Educators cannot afford to let their curricula fall out-of-date. The lag between the best that psychology can supply us and its introduction to teacher-education programs must be kept as small as possible. Perceptual psychology has been around since 1940, and what it has to offer teacher education is too important to ignore.

Helpful Concepts from Modern Psychology

Perceptual psychology does more than provide the educator with a view of man consistent with his philosophy and practice. It also offers a considerable body of content capable of helping teachers develop the kinds of beliefs about people characteristic of good teachers. Some of this content is derived from a perceptual interpretation of information about behavior which good teacher-education programs have included for many years. Some comes from the growing body of theory and research being developed by personalistic psychologists.

As we have previously pointed out, perceptual psychology does not require that we abandon prior approaches to the understanding of human behavior. The perceptual-humanistic view of behavior offers a new and broader frame of reference; it does not deny the tenets of the traditional stimulus-response approach. On the contrary, it *includes* that approach but goes beyond it to deal with problems the earlier approach could not adequately deal with. An analogy from mathematics may help to understand this: Arithmetic is a system of mathematics designed to deal with observable and countable events at a very simple level. Algebra, on the other hand, is a more advanced system of mathematics designed to deal with unknown numbers, events that must be inferred. Some mathematical problems can be solved simply by ordinary arithmetic. Others can be dealt with much more efficiently through algebraic techniques. There are even some problems that cannot be handled except by algebra. Humanistic-perceptual approaches to understanding behavior are like algebra. They enable us to move quickly and efficiently to vital understandings about human behavior without the laborious process of segmenting and mechanically describing minute behavioral events. Like algebra, also, they do not deny the validity of more primitive systems. They include and go beyond it.

Looking at the psychological content for new teachers from a perceptual orientation causes us to reaffirm some traditional material we have always found helpful, to eliminate some traditional material in favor of more auspicious concepts for teaching, and to add a number of new areas of investigation that hold much promise for the production of effective teachers.

The research on the perceptual organization of teachers discussed earlier suggests that good teachers typically perceive students as able, friendly, worthy, dependable, helpful, and internally motivated. Such beliefs about people may, of course, be acquired from one's own experience with them. The support of study, research, and psychological theory can make them more secure. Beliefs are more likely to serve as effective guides for behavior when they are consistent with the facts we have been able to acquire. This requires a consideration by young teachers of what is known about people from all points of view and the integration of this information into the student's own world of thinking and feeling

Extracting from the whole field of psychological thought those aspects most likely to be helpful to teachers, the authors have arrived at the list of topics indicated below. No doubt others would arrive at a different list.

Topics Chosen from Traditional and Perceptual Psychology Most Likely to Be Helpful in the Preparation of New Teachers

1. The nature of perception and its relation to behavior
   a. How we gather information about behavior
   b. The development of sensitivity to people
2. The nature and function of human need
   a. The origin of purposes
   b. The refinement of purpose into goals and values
   c. The effects of need, goals, and values on behavior
3. The self-concept
   a. What it is
   b. How it develops
   c. How it affects behavior
   d. How it changes
4. The adequate personality—goal of helping institutions
   a. The theory of self-actualization
   b. What such people are like
   c. How they grow and develop
   d. How inadequacies come about
5. The effect of the physical body on perceiving and behaving
   a. The effect of body structure on perceiving
   b. The basic principles of growth and development
6. The effect of the family and its relationships on the individual's perceptions of self and the world
   a. As source of learning about self and the world
   b. As product and transmitter of culture
   c. The problems of parents in our time
7. The effects of peer relationships on perceptions of self and the world
   a. The principles of group development and functioning
   b. The dynamics of group effects on individuals
8. How people learn
   a. Objective views of learning
   b. The relationship of emotion and affect to learning
   c. Humanistic views of learning

9. The nature of human capacities
    a. The limits of capacities
    b. How these limits develop
    c. How they may be changed
    d. The nature and nurture of creativity
10. The helping relationship
    a. The nature of such relationships
    b. The nature of helpers
    c. How helping relationships are established in a wide variety of settings
11. The nature of communication
    a. The nature and principles of communication
    b. The application of these principles to human interaction

This list of topics might be regarded as an outline for the content of a course in Educational Psychology or in the Psychological Foundations of Education. That, however, would be a great pity! Such topics ought not to be dealt with in a "course." The instructor may try to "cover" such topics, but what is needed is for the student teacher to "discover" their meaning and application. To assist the student in the process of personal discovery of meaning requires a program that allows such topics to be considered and reconsidered as the student teacher becomes more and more actively involved with children and other people. These opportunities should span the entire program of teacher preparation.

To help teachers develop accurate, useful beliefs about children and adults is not a one-shot matter. It requires consideration and reconsideration of the nature of people throughout the student's career and especially during his professional development. The perceptions characteristic of effective teachers are not superficial concepts. They are deeply rooted, ingrained beliefs, buttressed by knowledge, observation, and experience, and they find expression in all aspects of the good teacher's behavior. Such feelings are not acquired quickly or as a consequence of a single course. They come into being through a long, slow development involving the confrontation of ideas, to be sure, but even more important, through opportunities to discover meanings in interaction with colleagues, students, children, and the physical world.

The Importance of Meaning

The development of beliefs about people is also not learned from the meaningless accumulation and memorization of minutiae. It is not the details surrounding the topics listed above that teachers need to acquire, but the meaning attached to them. The evidence for the principle of maturation, for example, derived from experiments on bladder control or observations of the "ossification of the wrist bones" may be of intense interest to the scholar but contributes very little to the capacity of the practitioner to place the principle into effect.

Teachers need beliefs and understandings to be applied to particular persons, rather than hundreds of facts about people in the abstract. It is not enough that a teacher know the *facts* about human behavior—nor is it enough to be able to tell them to someone else else or to write out "good" answers on a test paper. The teacher's psychology must be a working psychology, a practitioner's psychology.

One can learn to drive a car even if one is not a mechanic. A mechanic may drive a car better, to be sure, but not enough to warrant our taking the time and energy to make mechanics out of all psychological principles. They do not need to be psychologists. There is a vast difference between understanding a *person* and understanding *about* him.

The Staff's and Students' Responsibility

For student teachers to acquire the kinds of beliefs characteristic of effective professional workers means that psychology and the problem of the nature of man must be an integral part of the curriculum throughout the college. The responsibility for helping students develop sensitivity cannot be relegated to a particular time, course, or faculty group. Every encounter between students and faculty in or out of the classroom contributes to learning. Students discover their values in interaction with significant people. Despite fine words and lofty sentiments, cynicism, dishonesty, and attitudes of contempt for others will not escape them. In the previous chapter we pointed out the importance of the attitudes of teachers in the content areas. How much more important it is that the professors students encounter in the professional aspects of their training should express the kinds of beliefs in people characteristic of effective teachers.

There are professors in teacher-education programs who teach democracy but who do not really believe that "free people can find their own best ways," or should be free at all. There are teachers who do not really think that students are worthy, supervisors who do not see teachers as able, and administrators so busy dealing with things they forget about persons. In thinking about teacher-education reform, it is easy to consider courses, regulations, and what to do about students. It is uncomfortable to face the fact that student beliefs are affected by our own. Uncomfortable as it may be, the fact is inescapable. Helping students to become effective teachers is a deeply personal problem, and the humanity and beliefs of the teacher-preparation faculty itself is a crucial factor in the process. Student teachers' beliefs about people are learned from the philosophy and values of their teachers, not just those who teach philosophy and psychology, but all of them, including the dean.

Sensitivity and Involvement

One of the characteristics of good teachers from the research reported in Chapter 2 is an internal, people-oriented frame of reference—a sensitivity to others. It is this sensitivity which the teacher-education program must develop in its students. Sensitivity is a matter of feelings, beliefs, and understandings, the ability to put oneself in the other fellow's shoes and to see the way things are with him. It is a matter of making inferences about how people think and feel and perceive and of checking these inferences against experience. Knowing a principle is but a first step toward understanding. Sensitivity comes only as students discover the deeper meaning of principles.

Sensitivity is an active thing. It cannot be learned at arm's length. Its development requires active involvement of self with people, the use of the teacher's own being as an instrument, as an observer and maker of inferences about people and their worlds. The development of sensitivity is a matter of commitment on the part of the staff and students alike. To learn what people are really like, students need the encounter of personal interaction with ideas and with people, both children and adults. This kind of involvement may be brought about in many ways. Some of these are suggested below, but the reader may devise others more suitable to his own peculiar tasks and personality. Almost any kind of encounter can have important learning values for the student, but, of course, some will be much more fruitful than others.

The Use of Observation for Developing Sensitivity

Perhaps the most time-honored device for developing sensitivity has been the use of observations. Most teacher-education programs require students to spend many hours observing the behavior of students or teachers. Many instructors put great faith in this technique despite the fact that student teachers often find it distasteful and a waste of time. This is unfortunate, but applying the principles of perceptual psychology may help us to see the problem in a new light. The authors are convinced that we have often made such experiences fruitless and frustrating for students because of a mistaken belief that observations must be made objectively.

Many have made such a fetish of objectivity in the making of observations that we have blinded students to the real meaning and values of observing. Because we want to develop in students "disciplined observation," to see what is *really* going on, we have insisted that they report exactly what occurred, precisely, and in detail. But one of the factors that determines perception is the intent of the perceiver, and students set to look at behavior in detail dutifully see it so and report it so. They are thus committed to a very dull task. Here, for example, is a portion of a lengthy observation report made by a student teacher:

> Jimmy picked up his pencil, examined the end of it. He got out of his seat and walked to the back of the room. He sharpened his pencil, looked out the window for a moment, and returned to his seat. On the way back to his seat, he tapped Joe on the head with the pencil as he passed him. He sat down and straightened his paper. He looked at the board where the teacher had placed the problem. He read the problem to himself. He sucked on the end of his pencil. He twisted his feet around the bottom of his desk, and then he started to write the answer. He worked very slowly and once in a while he would look up and around the room. Once he put his head down on his arm and wrote from that position. He looked up and saw Ed Price. He made a face at Ed and shrugged his shoulders. . . .

Is it any wonder that students often find this kind of reporting sheer drudgery? It is no surprise to us that they rebel at such busywork. They should. But this is not just a waste of time. Worse yet, it directs the student's attention to the wrong issues! For example, if the student is observing a teacher, the need for objectivity focuses his attention on the teacher's behavior or methods. But methods, as we have seen earlier, can never be comprehended as acts in themselves. Without consideration of the teacher's purposes and perceptions of self, students, and situation, objective reporting of what the teacher did is practically useless. Following this procedure, the student fails to understand the teacher on the one hand and looks in the wrong places for his own improvement on the other. In observing a child objectively, the student's attention is directed to behavior rather than causes. This leads naturally to a preoccupation with management rather than helping, controlling rather than facilitating. Children can rarely be understood from a consideration of their behavior alone. It is only as we comprehend its meaning to them that we find the key to working with them. Meanings, however, lie inside persons and cannot be observed directly. Yet, while meanings cannot be read directly, they can be inferred by a process of "reading behavior backwards." Such inferences are not made by coldly recording a series of specific behaviors in sequence and minute detail. They require that the observer use himself as an observation instrument by immersing himself in the situation.

Seeing the problem this way we have given up asking students to make detached factual observation reports. Instead, we ask students to become sensitive and interpretive of the meanings existing for the persons they are observing. In the case of Jimmy above, for example, we ask them, "What do you think he is trying to do?" "How do you suppose he feels?" "How would you have to feel to behave like that?" "How do you suppose he sees the teacher, the problem on the board, himself, the other kids?" and so on. This kind of empathic observation is more likely to help develop the kind of practitioner's psychology they need to work effectively with children.

Some kind of direct personal involvement with children prior to internship is encouraged in most teacher-education programs. Typically this includes limited forms of participation in the classroom or tutorial assignments. Ideally students ought to have opportunities for continuous contact with children inside as well as outside the classroom, since children are the raw material with which teachers must eventually work. Every person who has ever been a child himself has had some experience with children, and this ought to be capitalized on at the earliest possible moment. Beyond that we need to find ways of involving professional students in all kinds of settings, depending on what it is they are getting ready for. We have sometimes been fearful of turning students loose on children for fear they might do them some very great damage. The assignment of students to work with children must, of course, be done responsibly. On the other hand, modern psychologists assure us that children are far tougher than we have been accustomed to think. It takes a lot to destroy a child, and a single mistake is seldom likely to be permanently damaging. Professional students need to be willing to spend the time and energies required for continuous interactions with children. They also need to be willing to take the risk of making mistakes and have the courage to seek the staff's help in dealing with the problems they encounter. During the internship the student teacher has the best opportunity to apply the skills of empathic observation and inference making he has already developed in his previous encounters with children, as well as developing these skills more fully. But the development of sensitivity should be an active objective with as much involvement as possible at every level of preparation.

What students learn from such experiences can be immeasurably enhanced by effective teaching and supervision. Sensitivity seems most effectively learned when involvement is accompanied by, or followed as closely as possible by, opportunities to explore and consider the meaning of what was experienced. Many instructors are keenly aware of this principle and provide opportunities for the exploration of the meaning of experience through various types of group discussions designed to give students opportunities to kick ideas around and to test them against the interaction of others. Involvement can also be obtained from activities carried out alone, such as an individual research project or the writing of a paper. It may also occur in activities that do not bring people face to face. Having students write letters to the instructor about their reactions to their experiences, for example, often are extremely valuable both to the student and the instructor. Generally speaking, however, various forms of group discussion or individual interaction remain our most valuable means of inducing the exploration and discovery of meaning.

Best results are achieved when it is possible to combine observations and active involvement with children with immediate discussion in the excellent fashion described by Sarason[8] or in the kinds of discussion sessions advocated by Earl Kelley.[9] One of the great contributions of television to teacher education is the opportunities it provides to carry on observation and discussion simultaneously without disturbing teachers or pupils in the process.

Finally, sensitivity to others can be developed when students have opportunities to interact closely with their fellow students and with faculty. Sensitivity training and the guidelines and techniques for exploring and sharing personal goals and values suggested by Raths et al.[10] can be of immense help in these interpersonal encounters. Even plain "rap" sessions, planned or spontaneous, offer great benefits. To hear someone, to really listen, to tune in and be in touch with another person is a skill that takes time and can only be learned by interacting with people.

Whatever the techniques or kinds of personal encounter, student teachers need maximum opportunities to explore and discover accurate and workable understandings of what people are like and why they behave as they do. In this chapter we have looked at some of the ways students may be helped to acquire such beliefs from psychology and philosophy, from their experiences with their teachers, and from personal involvement with children and teachers. Beliefs about people are also acquired from the ways in which the student himself is treated, and that is the topic of our next chapter.

ENDNOTES

[1]A. W. Combs, "The Personal Approach to Good Teaching," *Educational Leadership* 21 (1964): 369–378.

[2]A. W. Combs et al., "Florida Studies in the Helping Professions," University of Florida Monographs, Social Sciences, no. 37 (Gainsville: University of Florida Press, 1969).

[3]Richard Usher and John Hanke, "The 'Third Force' in Psychology and College Teacher Effectiveness Research at the University of Northern Colorado," *Colorado Journal of Educational Research* 10, no. 2 (Winter 1971).

[4]Robert G. Brown, "A Study of Perceptual Organization of Elementary and Secondary 'Outstanding Young Educators,' " Unpublished Doctoral Dissertation (Gainsville: University of Florida, 1970).

[5]Herman G. Vonk, "The Relationship of Teacher Effectiveness to Perception of Self and Teaching Purposes," Unpublished Doctoral Dissertation (Gainsville: University of Florida, 1970).

[6]D. A. Dellow, "A Study of the Perceptual Organization of Teachers and Conditions of Empathy, Congruence, and Positive Regard," Unpublished Doctoral Dissertation (Gainsville: University of Florida, 1971).

[7]Charles Van Loan Dedrick, "The Relationship Between Perceptual Characteristics and Effective Teaching at the Junior College Level," Unpublished Doctoral Dissertation (Gainsville: University of Florida, 1972).

[8]S. B. Sarason, K. Davidson, and B. Blott, *The Preparation of Teachers* (New York: Wiley, 1962).

[9]E. C. Kelley, *The Workshop Way of Learning* (New York: Harper, 1951).

[10]E. Louis Raths, Merrill Harmin, and Sidney B. Simon, *Values and Teaching* (Columbus: Charles E. Merrill, 1966).

6

The Self of the Effective Teacher

The essence of successful professional work is the effective use of self. This personal quality of professional preparation has already been recognized in the training of doctors, counselors, nurses, social workers, pastors, and psychotherapists. It is equally true for the training of teachers. The good teacher is first and foremost a person. That "person-ness" is the vehicle through which he accomplishes whatever he does as a teacher.

What is more, the process of learning itself is a matter of personal exploration and discovery. A program of teacher education that has not affected its students in personal ways has failed its mission. The effective teacher must *be* somebody. He is not a passive baby-sitter meekly following instructions, guiding students through steps and processes in which he is not involved. Neither does he hide behind his subject matter and pour out objective facts like a robot. Good teaching involves personal interaction. The process of teacher education must be as student-centered as modern philosophy demands the teaching occurring everywhere else in our schools should be.

WHAT KIND OF SELF FOR EFFECTIVE TEACHING?

The Capacity for Sharing Self

The production of a professional worker calls for the ability to share self on the one hand and to discipline self on the other. The teacher's willingness and ability to enter into relationships with students, colleagues, and subject matter is crucial to effective teaching. This calls for qualities of openness, of "making one's self visible." The individual must be willing to disclose himself and to permit other people to see him as he is, to know what he thinks, believes, and stands for. This personal quality of interaction is basic to communication. We do not listen to nonentities and we do not hear lightweights.

Communication between teacher and students improves when students respect the teacher. A teacher has two kinds of authority. One is "unearned" authority; the other is "earned." The two are different. A teacher's "unearned" authority comes with his teaching assignment. When he starts the school year with a new class of students, all he has at first is his "unearned" authority: He is the assigned boss of the class. He may have the reputation of being a good teacher who "understands kids," "is fair," "knows his stuff," and so on, but neither the power vested in his role nor the best reputation will lead automatically to genuine communication between teacher and students. Such communication comes about and increases in direct proportion to the degree of "earned" authority, that is, the authority the students *themselves* invest in the teacher as a result of their personal discovery of who this teacher is, what he believes and stands for, and how he operates.

The Adequate Personality

The giving of self called for in helping professions like teaching is probably possible only in the degree to which the helper himself feels basically fulfilled. Being oneself not only improves communication with students, it is also important for the teacher's mental health. One of the authors once overheard a colleague say, "I can hardly wait until vacation so I can be a person." What a dreadful way to live for a teacher who tries to act out a role 185 days a year, year-in and year-out! A deeply deprived self cannot afford to give itself away. A self must possess a satisfactory degree of adequacy before it can venture commitment and encounter. As Earl Kelley has expressed it, people must feel that "they are enough".[1] A small, weak self cannot behave in ways that risk further diminution.

The question of what constitutes an adequate self has intrigued a number of psychologists in recent years. They have tried to discover just what such people would be like. Some of these writers have referred to the "fully functioning self," "self-actualization," "self-realization," "the adequate personality," and "high-level wellness." By whatever name they have approached the question, however, all are asking, "What kind of person would it be who was truly achieving the utmost of his potentialities and at the same time contributing effectively to the welfare of his fellow human beings?" Approaching this question from the perceptual point of view, highly adequate personalities seem to be characterized by four general qualities:[2,3]

1. They tend to see themselves in essentially positive ways. That is to say, they see themselves as generally liked, wanted, successful, able persons of dignity, worth, and integrity.
2. They perceive themselves and their world accurately and realistically. These people do not kid themselves. They are able to confront the world with openness and acceptance, seeing both themselves and external events with a minimum of distortion or defensiveness.

3. They have deep feelings of identification with other people. They feel "at one with" large numbers of persons of all kinds and varieties. This is not simply a surface manifestation of "liking people" or being a "hail-fellow-well-met" type of person. Identification is not a matter of polished social graces, but a feeling of oneness in the human condition.
4. They are well informed. Adequate people are not stupid. They have perceptual fields that are rich, varied, and available for use when needed.

In the 1962 ASCD Yearbook, *Perceiving, Behaving, Becoming*,[4] a national committee of educators explored what the concept of the adequate personality meant for educational practice. They came to the conclusion that the production of such persons is the very goal of education and that the above qualities of self-actualization provide important guidelines for educational practice. These criteria are equally important for determining the kinds of teachers we would like to produce. Where else in our society is it more important that adequate persons be in command than in guiding and encouraging youth?

In the "Florida Studies in the Helping Professions"[5] and in more recent studies on effective teachers done in Florida and elsewhere,[6,7,8,9,10] the characteristics below were found to be associated with effective helping. Good teachers, like good counselors and ministers, typically perceive themselves in the following ways:

1. Good teachers feel identified with, rather than apart from, others. The good teacher tends to see himself as a part of all mankind; he sees himself as identified with people rather than as withdrawn, removed, apart, or alienated from others.
2. Good teachers feel basically adequate rather than inadequate. The good teacher generally sees himself as enough; as having what is needed to deal with his problems. He does not see himself as lacking and as unable to cope with problems.

3. Good teachers feel trustworthy rather than untrustworthy. The good teacher has trust in his own organism. He sees himself as essentially dependable, reliable, as having the potentiality for coping with events as opposed to seeing self in a tentative fashion with doubts about the potentiality and reliability of the organism.
4. Good teachers see themselves as wanted rather than unwanted. The good teacher sees himself as essentially likeable, attractive (in the personal, not physical, appearance sense), wanted, and in general capable of bringing forth a warm response from those people important to him, as opposed to feeling ignored, unwanted, or rejected by others.
5. Good teachers see themselves as worthy rather than unworthy. The good teacher sees himself as a person of consequence, dignity, integrity, and worthy of respect as opposed to being a person of little consequence who can be overlooked, discounted, whose dignity and integrity do not matter.

It is apparent that these characteristics of effective teachers and other helpers tally closely with the qualities of the adequate personality indicated above. If these are the characteristics of good teachers, then it follows that these are the perceptual characteristics we need to produce in the professional education of teachers.

The Capacity for Disciplining Self

Although teaching is a deeply personal matter, it is not a self-indulgent one. The purpose of teaching is service; its primary goal is the growth of self in the student, not the teacher. This is a goal often lost sight of, particularly by college teachers addicted to lecturing. As one student put it, commenting on his college frustrations, "I always thought college was for the nourishment of the student, but I was wrong. College exists for the enhancement of the professor!"

While self-disclosure is necessary for communication, self-discipline is equally called for. Good teaching is not maudlin. Teachers must have the dignity, integrity, and capacity to set self aside long enough to minister to the needs of others. This is not easy for the beginning teacher. It is a difficult thing to set aside one's own needs. Most of us can do this only for very short periods and then only by dint of considerable conscious, careful effort.

Whether an individual is able to set self aside in the manner required for self-discipline will also depend on the degree of personal adequacy he feels. It is only when persons feel fundamentally adequate that self can be transcended and attention given to the needs of others. Inadequate persons cannot afford the time and effort required to assist others as long as they feel deprived themselves. "Selfishness" is characteristic of maladjustment and inadequacy.

It is a fascinating thing that the necessity for "coping" with life becomes greatly reduced in the experience of adequate persons. Maslow, for example, points out that all of us have two kinds of behaviors: (1) those things we do in order to cope with life and (2) those kinds of behaviors that are simply expressive behaviors carried out as fulfillments or expressions of ourselves.[11] Adequate personalities, interestingly enough, show far less coping behavior and much more expressive behavior than other people. Apparently, in simply expressing themselves, they manage to deal effectively with the world without the necessity for giving such problems much attention. Just by being who he is, the adequate personality achieves what the inadequate one must work at. Self-discipline is not a conscious effort for such persons but a natural consequence of an internal state. The teacher who feels fundamentally adequate can and will give of himself, automatically, without the necessity for working at it.

In the light of these understandings, helping students to become good teachers is in part synonymous with helping them to become personalities. It follows that teacher-education programs must assist students in every way to greater experiences of self-fulfillment. Programs must be oriented toward the production of at least the criteria for adequacy we have indicated above. In addition to helping students be well informed, which we have always sought, we need further to aid students to perceive themselves in positive ways, to confront themselves and the world with openness and acceptance, and to develop a deep sense of identification with the human condition.

PRODUCING TEACHERS WITH ADEQUATE PERSONALITIES

The Selection Program

One way of acquiring teachers who see themselves and others in adequate ways is to select them. Everyone has numerous ways of seeing himself, acquired from the experience of living. These beliefs may be accurate and helpful or inaccurate and confusing, but no one can operate in the world we live in without a conception of himself and what other people are like. Professional education, then, is not a matter of teaching people to perceive something entirely new and unique. Rather, it is a question of helping people to change the perceptions they already have or to discover new and deeper meanings of already existing concepts. There are some lucky people whose life experiences have already taught them to perceive themselves and others in ways that at the very start are superior to the concepts some of their fellow students will only achieve by the end of the program. It is literally true that some people do not need special training to make them good teachers. Unhappily, the number of such persons is small and most people still need help. So we shall, no doubt, need teacher-preparation programs for a long time to come.

Theoretically, of course, it s possible to make almost anyone into a good teacher, given the time and the necessary program. Practically, however, the attempt to make just anyone into an effective teacher is too wasteful to consider. A teacher-training program must weigh the cost of its program not only in dollars and cents but also in terms of the most efficient use of the time and energies of its faculty and the time and anguish of its students. The prospects for a teacher-education program might be divided into three groups:

1. Those who already possess a considerable measure of the perceptual qualities of the good teacher we have indicated in these discussions.
2. Those who have a fair degree of these conceptual qualities and wto seem likely to profit from professional education.
3. Those who have very little of such perceptual organization and seem likely to change only slowly.

The first of these groups we need to recruit into our profession as rapidly as possible. The third group will require so much time, effort, and expense as to make the task too inefficient. These people should probably be helped to explore other alternatives. From the middle group we need to accept as many as possible, working down from the top until we have filled our facilities to capacity.

The Inadequacy of Objective Data. Most of us approach the business of selection with a great deal of apprehension. We do not want to hurt people, and we are worried that our unsupported human judgments may be inaccurate. As a consequence we usually select students on the basis of indications of academic aptitude derived from past records and tests of academic ability. Some teacher-preparation programs have added to this, very tentatively, judgments about personality and adjustment and and even sometimes a personal interview. When these latter criteria have been added, it has usually been with apologies. We feel vaguely guilty about using such "nonscientific," subjective criteria even though heavy reliance on objectively measured criteria boomerangs to destroy the very goals we seek.

We live in a world dominated by the "scientific method. " Daily, we are provided with apparent proof of the superiority of controlled measurement over freewheeling human observation. We are impressed, and we have a right to be. Wherever these devices are applicable to our problems, we certainly should use them. But science has become a sacred cow in our generation, and there is a seductive comfort in numbers. It is reassuring to be able to substantiate our own judgments by the apparently infallible statistic or written record. Accordingly, records of past behavior and the results of batteries of tests are given tremendous weight in selecting students. Sometimes, unhappily, they are even used exclusively.

In this book we have been describing the adequate teacher in perceptual terms. Neither records of past behavior nor test results, however, can be relied on at this stage of our knowledge to provide us with the information we need about human perceptions. Tests of academic aptitude can tell us something about the individual's probable success in acquiring subject matter. They tell us very little about the kinds of perceptual organization we want to know about in judging probable success in teaching.

The Need for Subjective Judgments. Perceptual psychologists have found out a great deal about how to explore the nature of perceptions but need to continue efforts in developing simple measuring devices to get at these aspects of human personality. This is an area in which we need more research. Meanwhile, if we are to improve our selective processes, it will be necessary for us to accept human judgments, values, and feelings as valid data upon which to make decisions. From the numerous studies on effective helpers cited previously, we are encouraged about the usefulness of subjective judgments for assessing a person's perceptions. Of course we will make some mistakes. This need not worry us unduly, however. No evaluation of a person's characteristics is ever infallible. Even the most rigorously "objective" measurement devices so far invented have considerable error built into them. As Combs has written elsewhere:

> The objective methods of science provide us with important checks on human observation and with logical presumption of greater accuracy when we use them. But, human judgment is all we have to depend upon in the absence of objective devices. We cannot shrink from confronting our pressing problems for lack of precision tools. We must do what we can with what we have. Persons who never used judgment would be forever confined to

> what was immediately palpable and observable. Judgment frees us to go beyond mere observation. To reject it as a tool for assessment is to limit ourselves to the least important aspects of our educational effort and so assures the increasing irrelevance of a system already desperately ill of that disease.
>
> The belief that judgment is somehow unscientific is an illusion. All science, of whatever description, is dependent upon human judgment. Science, itself, is merely a device to refine and control human judgment. The goal is not its elimination but its effective and efficient use. Judgment requires the use of the "observer as instrument" and, of course, this instrument, like any other in scientific use, must be properly calibrated to make sure its readings are as reliable as we can possibly make them. That can be done.[12]

Men have always had to proceed on the basis of the very best judgments they could make when they did not have other measures to work with. We may not wish to make such judgments, but we cannot avoid doing so. A professional worker is a person whose judgment can be relied on. It is this quality of judgment that separates professional work from mechanical work. Only the profession can judge the effectiveness of its members.[13,14] Excluding human judgment and experience from decision making only compounds the error of accepting objective data uncritically, especially when such data are not really related to our problems. Every profession that deals with human beings must make its most important decisions on the basis of judgments that cannot be set in numerical form. Teaching is a profession dependent on human values, and these must be accepted as valid data for our operations. In our experience in teaching and selecting students we find that most of our failures have been in those instances when we have succumbed to the belief that the statistics must surely be right and our own judgment wrong.

Human judgment is what we must use at every phase of our normal existence. The improvement of human judgment is what education is all about. The very essence of good teaching is the intelligent, creative use of human judgment.

Personal change is not an objective problem; it is a subjective one. Objective analysis of self has been vastly overrated as a device for personality change. Effective changes in self are not brought about by picking at the self. This practice can even be highly destructive.

CHANGING CONCEPTS OF SELF

Changes in behavior, including changes in one's personality, are most effectively brought about, not by introspection and analysis, but through slow changes in perceptions about outside events, and their relation to the self. To produce a change in a person's self requires a new experience that helps him to perceive himself in a different way. This may be brought about in at least three ways:

1. Through a direct provision of experience as, for example, when a child is aided through remedial reading to discover that he really can read after all, or a student teacher comes to believe he *can* teach as a result of a series of successful experiences.
2. As a consequence of perceiving an event in a new perspective. Some teachers have been so thoroughly indoctrinated with the idea that children are delicate and anything they do may ruin a child that when they make a mistake in handling a youngster, they are filled with remorse and conclude they are failures. Helping such teachers understand the really tough character of children and the genesis of maladjustment in more realistic terms permits the teacher to assess himself in more accurate terms.
3. Self-perception may change following changed perception of others. For example, the teacher who comes to see children more accurately and realistically behaves more effectively in dealing with them. As a consequence his efforts are more successful, others perceive him and act toward him as a more successful teacher, and the teaching self-concept changes accordingly so he sees himself as a better teacher. A change in the perception

of others thus causes them to behave in ways that change the perception of self. The self is learned from the looking glass held up for us by others.

These principles provide us with clues to what the teacher-education program must do to produce more effective concepts of self in its students. Since the self-concept of the teacher is learned in the same fashion as any other perception, the conditions for learning discussed in an earlier chapter are equally relevant here. Teacher-educators must concern themselves with

1. Creating an atmosphere in the college and within its classrooms and activities that encourages and facilitates the student's discovery of himself as a more adequate person and teacher.
2. Providing experiences designed to help students see themselves as adequate, effective people.
3. Assisting actively the student's personal search for meaning and the discovery of himself as a person and as a teacher.

Within the framework for learning, what kinds of experiences shall educators provide in order to assure the development of adequate and effective teachers? The guidelines are plainly set before us. They may be found in current thinking about the nature of the adequate person and in the research on good teaching mentioned earlier.

Adequate personalities, say the perceptual psychologists, are people who see themselves in positive ways: as liked, wanted, acceptable, and able. So do good teachers. But these definitions of desirable perceptual qualities are more than definitions of goodness. They provide the criteria in terms of which we may select the kinds of experiences we need in order to produce more adequate teachers.

Fallacy of Self-analysis

If it is true that good teachers see themselves as liked, wanted, acceptable, and able, then these are the kind of personal perceptions the teacher-education program must produce. How is this to be done? At first glance it would seem logical that the way to go about producing a change in the self-concept would be to examine one's self critically, decide how he wished to be different, do whatever was necessary to accomplish that, then reexamine one's self to see how far he had come. This is the typical behavioral-objectives, performance-based criteria approach to change in education currently fashionable. It seems straightforward and businesslike. Unfortunately, it does not work very well applied to people.

The impression that self-analysis is a valuable device for getting people to change themselves is largely inaccurate because it focuses attention on the wrong aspects of the problem. One does not come to feel he is a more lovable person by sitting around thinking about his lovableness! People discover they are more or less lovable from the reactions of persons around them, and the way to become more lovable requires behaving in more loving ways. That does not call for looking at how one feels about himself; it requires thinking about how one feels about the *people out there:* one's friends, colleagues, family, acquaintances, students, or whatever. The self-concept, it must be understood, is not something one *decides* to be; it is the product of the feedback we get from the world around us, especially those persons who seem to us to be important—what psychologists call significant others. One learns he is likeable from being liked, or learns he is acceptable from having been accepted.

Producing Positive Self-concepts

For the teachers' college, the path to producing changed self-concepts in students is to treat students so. People learn that they are liked, wanted, acceptable, and able from experiences of having been treated that way by the people around them and from successful experiences that teach them they are able. Teacher-education students take their self-concepts with them wherever they go, and every experience they have makes its contribution pro or con in building or tearing down self-perceptions. Helping to build up students' self-concepts is a responsibility of every member of the teacher-preparation faculty. It cannot be set aside as the exclusive task of any special group. Each staff member has his effect on the self-concepts of students whether he wants to or not. The only thing he can control is whether his impact on the student will be positive, negative, or of no account whatever.

In similar fashion, the attitudes of self-acceptance and openness to experience, characteristic of adequate persons and effective teachers, are the consequence of successful experiences in this realm. One learns to accept oneself from having been accepted by significant people. Openness to experience is learned in part from positive feelings about self that make risk-taking possible and partly from association with open, courageous persons. A teacher-preparation faculty is no place for timid souls.

So, too, feelings of commitment, encounter, and oneness with the human condition are learned in the process of growing up from those around us. It follows that teacher-educators must contribute to student feelings of belonging and must provide an atmosphere of compassion and concern for people from which feelings of identification can be acquired.

The characteristics of adequate personalities and the perceptual characteristics of effective professional workers are not inherent qualities. They are learned, and what is learned can be taught. Research on the nature of adequacy has pointed the way. It remains for teacher-educators to set about the business of achieving such ways of seeing self in students with greater efficiency if we are to meet our responsibilities to the next generations.

How shall we do it? For the authors to attempt to spell out in detail what needs to be done in order to put these principles into effect would be presumptuous indeed. This is not an objective to be assigned to a particular course. Nor is it a matter for any individual to decide. It is a matter for education faculties to address themselves to in whatever ways are appropriate in the light of their local purposes and conditions.

It must involve all aspects of the program and all members of the staff, beginning with a belief that "people are important," then formulating plans and procedures to provide the kinds of experiences that will assure the production of teachers with the perceptual organization of effective professional workers. In the characteristics of the adequate personality outlined for us by perceptual psychology, and in the research on the nature of the self of good teachers, we have a yardstick for a critical appraisal of current practices on the one hand and guidelines for the development of new practices on the other.

A good beginning in this direction was suggested more than a decade ago in the 1962 ASCD Yearbook, *Perceiving, Behaving, Becoming.*[15] In this volume a committee of teachers who wrote the yearbook systematically examined educational practices that impede or encourage (1) the positive view of self, (2) self-acceptance and the accurate view of self, (3) creativity and openness to experience, and (4) the feeling of identification. The work of these educators has attracted much attention among public school teachers and curriculum workers. Most of what they had to say is equally applicable to problems of teacher education. More recently these ideas and concepts have been amplified in other writings.[16, 17, 18, 19, 20] A most recent attempt to implement these concerns in the development of teacher-education programs has been made at the University of Florida.[21] This new program of teacher education has been operating successfully for several years and will be discussed more fully in a later chapter.

THE STUDENT COUNSELING PROGRAM

A professional program oriented around the personality of the teacher must maintain steady contact with its students. If teachers-in-training are to take greater responsibilities for their own learning, and if the learning program is to be continually adjusted to student readiness, machinery must be established to provide for the kind of personal contact that will make such a program possible. This calls for an effective counseling program.[22] It would be ideal if all members of the faculty could do a good job of counseling with students and would regard this as an important aspect of their jobs. Such a millennium, however, has not yet been reached, and it is probably unrealistic to expect this of any faculty. What is needed is to make adjustments in terms of faculty responsibilities, competencies, and interests with respect to counseling to make the most effective use of those who possess counseling talents.

A professional program oriented around student growth will need to help students continually to review, evaluate, and plan for further activities. This kind of personal interest should be provided for all students. It can best be given by those members of the staff who have continuing contacts with students and who like this kind of personal contact, those who can take an interest in students and relate to them in warm and friendly fashion. The training of a counselor is not a mysterious laying-on-of-hands procedure. It is a matter of helping an individual to make effective use of himself in face-to-face relationships. Good teachers usually make good counselors. Beginning with such personnel, the counseling procedures of any teacher-education program can often be greatly improved by a comparatively simple course of in-service training. All that is needed is an instructor who knows his business and who is interested in improving his techniques and understanding in the field of counseling.

Since becoming a teacher is a highly personal thing, the teacher-preparation counseling program also needs to give more intensive personal counseling than that ordinarily provided by instructors and advisers. A student's capacity to use himself as an effective instrument will depend in large part on his personal happiness and freedom from psychological distress. There is ample reason for advocating a program of counseling for students solely on the basis of its desirability for personal and human reasons. It is even more desirable in professional education. In a business like teaching, above all, we need adequate, healthy personalities, and it is a responsibility of the teacher-training institution to bring about this end as effectively and as positively as it can. There is ample evidence to demonstrate a relationship between the mental health of teachers and students. But even if this were not so, the effect of unhappiness and inadequacy on the sheer productivity and efficiency of teachers should be enough to convince us of the importance of personal counseling during the student's training days.

The provision of personal counseling for students is, of course, expensive. Schools are also hesitant at times to assume responsibility for this aspect of the student's life. It is often argued that in a society not yet ready to assume the financial burdens of this kind of service, the college can accept only very limited responsibility for the personal adjustment of students. This argument may have some validity in the training of engineers, physicists, mathematicians, and scholars in the various disciplines. Surely it does not apply in the preparation of teachers, the people to whom we entrust major responsibility for the health and welfare of our youth. A profession whose business is to produce adequate people must ensure that its ranks are filled by people who can carry out that responsibility and who are themselves the most adequate people we can find. The personal qualities of the teacher are so important that a professional training program must either help its students to become the most effective people they can be or help them to leave the profession as gracefully as possible. A professional program which ignores this facet of training must necessarily be less efficient than is desirable.

Fortunately, not all students need personal counseling. One of the tasks of an effective selection system should be to make certain of the basic health of students entering the program. If selection is effective, a teacher-education program should not be saddled with very many cases requiring deep counseling. Most personal counseling does not require extensive psychiatric service. While any school will, of course, have occasional students who need deep psychiatric care, the vast majority can be helped by counseling of a much less intensive sort. Nonmedical counselors of very high quality are now being produced in increasing numbers by schools of social work, psychology, counseling, and guidance. The presence of counselors on a college staff can often make important contributions to the program in other than their purely counseling roles. In fact, it is probably unwise to assign counselors to full-time counseling practice. It is much better to utilize the many important teaching functions which can be carried out by such personnel for part of their time so that they become recognized as an integral part of the faculty.

ENDNOTES

[1]Earl C. Kelley, "The Fully Functioning Self," in A. W. Combs, ed., *Perceiving, Behaving, Becoming: A New Focus for Education*, 1962 ASCD Yearbook (Washington, D.C.: Association for Supervision and Curriculum Development, 1962).

[2]A. W. Combs and Donald Snygg, *Individual Behavior* (New York: Harper, 1959).

[3]A. W. Combs, ed., *Perceiving, Behaving, Becoming: A New Focus For Education*, 1962 ASCD Yearbook (Washington, D.C.: Association for Supervision and Curriculum Development, 1962).

[4]Ibid.

[5]A. W. Combs et al., "Florida Studies in the Helping Professions," University of Florida Monographs, Social Sciences, no. 37 (Gainsville: University of Florida Press, 1969).

[6]Robert G. Brown, "A Study of Perceptual Organization of Elementary and Secondary 'Outstanding Young Educators,' " Unpublished Doctoral Dissertation (Gainsville: University of Florida, 1970).

[7]Herman G. Vonk, "The Relationship of Teacher Effectiveness to Perception of Self and Teaching Purposes," Unpublished Doctoral Dissertation (Gainsville: University of Florida, 1970).

[8]D. A. Dellow, "A Study of the Perceptual Organization of Teachers and Conditions of Empathy, Congruence, and Positive Regard," Unpublished Doctoral Dissertation (Gainsville: University of Florida, 1971).

[9]Richard Usher and John Hanke, "The 'Third Force' in Psychology and College Teacher Effectiveness Research at the University of Northern Colorado," *Colorado Journal of Educational Research* 10, no. 2 (Winter, 1971).

[10]Charles Van Loan Dedrick, "The Relationship Between Perceptual Characteristics and Effective Teaching at the Junior College Level," Unpublished Doctoral Dissertation (Gainsville: University of Florida, 1972).

[11]A. H. Maslow, *Motivation and Personality* (New York: Harper, 1954).

[12]A. W. Combs, *Educational Accountability: Beyond Behavioral Objectives* (Washington, D.C.: Association for Supervision and Curriculum Development, 1972).

[13]A. W. Combs, "Can We Measure Good Teaching Objectively?" *N.E.A. Journal* 53 (1964): 34–36+.

[14]See G. W. Denemark, ed., *Criteria for Curriculum Decisions in Teacher Education* (Washington, D.C.: Association for Supervision and Curriculum Development, 1964) for an excellent review of the problem of selection and suggestions for selection programs.

[15]A. W. Combs, *Teacher Education: A Problem in Becoming.* In AACTE and AST Partnership in Teacher Education (Washington, D.C.: American Association of Colleges for Teacher Education, 1968).

[16]A. W. Combs, D. L. Avila, and W. W. Purkey, *Helping Relationships: Basic Concepts for the Helping Professions* (Boston: Allyn and Bacon, 1971).

[17]*Steps Toward Excellence in Teacher Education: Reports from Around the Country* (Washington, D.C., American Association of Colleges for Teacher Education, October 1971).

[18]Carl K. Rogers and William R. Coulson, eds., *Freedom to Learn*, (Columbus: Charles E. Merrill, 1969).

[19]Christopher Jencks and David Riesman, *The Academic Revolution* (New York: Doubleday, 1968).

[20]George Leonard, *Education and Ecstasy* (New York: Delacorte Press, 1968).

[21]Robert Blume, "Humanizing Teacher Education," *Phi Delta Kappan* (March 1971).

[22]Denemark, op. cit.

7

The Teacher's Purposes

How teachers behave in the classroom, the faculty meeting, the teachers' convention, or sitting at home before the television is determined in large measure by the purposes they seek to fulfill in each instance. In Chapter 1 we defined the effective teacher as one who has learned to use himself effectively in carrying out his own and society's purposes. The teacher who is confused about what he is trying to do creates confusion in his students and is very likely to fail in accomplishing either his own or society's objectives.

In recent years American public schooling has been severely criticized for what Charles Silberman in his book, *Crisis in the Classroom*, has called "mindlessness . . . the failure of people at every level to ask why they are doing what they are doing or to inquire into the consequences."[1] When purposes are confused or misdirected, behavior is too. Worse still, confusion of purpose makes it almost impossible for other people to deal with the teacher and is an important cause of teacher failure. Students can, after all, only deal with a teacher in terms of the expectancies they have come to feel are characteristic of him. If the teacher's values and purposes are confused, then the student is left groping around in the dark in his attempt to find a way of working effectively with his teacher. To avoid this kind of confusion, young teachers have often been admonished to "be consistent." Such advice is seldom likely to be helpful, however, because it is directed to the wrong goal. Consistency does not lie in the repetitive character of behavior. It is a function of the stability and clarity of the individual's beliefs about what is important and worth doing. The beliefs teachers hold about what is important determine what they respond to and what methods they choose to deal with matters.

Society's or the administration's purposes will only be given effective expression if, somehow, they have become a part of the personal purposes of the teacher for it is only personal purposes that are likely to find their way into expression in the classroom situation. No matter how well a teacher may have learned to give the "right" answers and say the "right" things, when the classroom door is shut there is no one but the pupils and the teacher to decide what is to be done. Good teaching calls for healthy purposes capable of producing behavior in the best interests of everyone: teacher, pupil, and society itself.

THE PURPOSES OF EFFECTIVE TEACHERS

As we have seen, a good teacher is one who has learned to use his self effectively and efficiently. Whether he can do this well will in turn be dependent on the belief systems he has developed. What makes a "professional" different from a "nonprofessional" is that—presumably because of his training, experience, special knowledge, or discipline—he is able to provide better answers to problems. Professional teachers are not mindless, haphazardly trying what "might" work. They are responsible persons who do whatever they do for good and defensible reasons. Their actions are guided by purpose and goal.

That people behave in terms of their purposes is hardly news to most of us. We are keenly aware that, that is true with respect to our own behavior. And as we look at our friends we quickly discover that their purposes are so important that it becomes possible for us to predict their behavior with considerable accuracy. But what kinds of purposes do good teachers seek fulfillment for? As with human beings generally, teachers' purposes vary greatly from person to person. Some will be as specific as "Jimmy Smith should see the difference between ph and f." Others will be more general, like "helping children develop to the maximum of their potentialities." Some will be social and philosophical, like "understanding democracy." Still others will be highly individual, as, for example, "helping Jimmy Smith catch up in reading" or personal, as when a teacher says, "I love the feeling I get when a youngster responds to me so."

Since all behavior is purposive, all the teacher's beliefs are important in determining his behavior. But some, of course, are more directly related to his professional functioning than others. Among the purposes especially significant for the effective teacher, will be, at least, the following:

Beliefs about the Basic Nature of Man

It makes a great deal of difference whether one believes human beings are basically good or evil, trustworthy or untrustworthy, striving for power, freedom, or self-actualization. Throughout history men have always behaved toward one another on the basis of such conceptions. The "doctrine of original sin," for example, held that human beings were basically perverse, conceived in sin, and somehow had to be saved from their own base nature. It is not surprising, then, that the schools created by people with such beliefs were pretty grim, cheerless places; salvation, itself, was at stake. But when people believed that man's misbehavior was due to being "possessed of the devil," folks felt sorry for the parents of an incorrigible child or assumed the parents had such a misfortune visited on them as punishment for their own wickedness. Vestiges of these concepts can still be seen in the attitudes of some people even in our own time.

Concepts of man continue to emerge in our time as well as in the past. In former times conceptions of man and his striving came mostly from religious bases. Some still do. These have been joined in our time by many perspectives from literature, philosophy, and the social sciences like sociology, anthropology, and psychology. The field is immensely richer and the choices far more numerous than formerly, but the effect of belief on action is still the same; teachers in the process of becoming must arrive at some position. If they do not do so consciously they will do so unconsciously. Either way their behavior will mirror the beliefs and determine the directions they take, the goals they seek, and the outcomes of their professional activities.

Beliefs about the Nature of Society and the Directions It Ought to Be Moving In

Regardless of how eloquent and well thought out teachers' purposes, unless they are ultimately related to the world community, they are necessarily inadequate. This emphatically does not mean that teachers' purposes need be in accord with any particular doctrine of world order. It does mean that, in the formulation of educational purposes that seem appropriate and morally defensible, teachers must regard themselves not as human isolates, but as educators-in-society. Teachers must be aware of and sensitive to social needs and desires. It is also necessary that teachers, discharging their obligations in a democratic manner, must always be something other than sycophants of those who wield power. If professional educators' purposes are authentic, they cannot put themselves in the unprofessional position of being dictated to by external social forces.

Teachers are in large part products of society in their own growing up, agents of society in their professional role, and makers and shapers of society as teachers and citizens. As such, the beliefs they hold about society's purposes and goals and the dreams they dream of the "good society" to be sought are matters of vital importance, not only to the society they live in and serve but also because they are crucial to teachers' professional successes and their personal fulfillment.

Beliefs about the Purposes of Education

What a teacher believes is the purpose of education in our society inevitably affects the goals he seeks and the techniques he employs in the classroom. How he behaves toward the "slow learner," for example, will be markedly affected by whether the teacher believes the purpose of education is: "to train the leaders of the future," "fit students into their proper social occupational roles," "induct students into the way of life of our society," or "help each child achieve the maximum of his potential."

Historically, in our society, as in most, the institution of education has been regarded as a major vehicle for preserving and perpetuating the cultural status quo. To this end the public schools have been expected to prepare youth to become "productive" citizens (intelligent voters, reliable breadwinners, responsible consumers, and the like). In discharging these responsibilities the teacher has been expected to facilitate the student's efficient and effective assumption of a societal role. In these times of dynamic change, however, no one, most assuredly the educator, can possibly know with any precision what roles the student will need to assume in his adult life. We simply cannot forecast well the kinds of problems our students will be called on to solve. Values, beliefs, art forms, laws—all cultural manifestations evolve with time so that the future cannot be defined in terms of the past or present.

More recently we have come to understand that the productive citizen of the future must be able to adapt intelligently to unforeseeable change. He must also be equipped to help induce that sociocultural change which thoughtful reflection indicates. This general problem-solving disposition is not merely a cool, dispassionate, cognitive function. It also requires tender, caring, loving attitudes.

It is not always easy to reconcile one's perceived teaching purposes with institutional demands. The educational institution, like all others, is appreciably affected by political power considerations and the becoming teacher will have to deal with these, too, as he formulates his personal sense of the appropriate purposes of school in our society. To help students acquire such rudders, the teachers' college will need to provide broad opportunities for exploration and personal discovery.

Beliefs about More Immediate Purposes in One's Own School, Subject Matter, and Classroom

Closer, more specific purposes related to the teacher's more immediate tasks and relationships will also govern how he uses himself as an instrument from day to day and moment to moment. Among these will be such understandings as the value and function of whatever content he is teaching, the local problems and responsibilities of the school in which he is working, and the particular purposes, long range and short, appropriate to the teacher's own classroom students or relationships.

The Teacher's Own Personal Purposes

A teacher is not only a "professional," he is also a unique flesh and blood human being with wants, desires, goals, hopes, fears, and aspirations quite aside from his professional role. These, too, have inescapable effects upon what goes on in the classroom. It makes a good deal of difference, what one's motives for being a teacher are. Is one teaching because: He loves the feeling of power and control? He needs to make a living and this is the best way he can find? He loves working with kids? Or he enjoys being an actor and commanding center stage? Since a teacher is a person his personal purposes come right along with him to class and play their part in determining what goes on there. In the helping professions of counseling and social work much time is spent in aiding the young practitioner to discover and understand his personal needs and "hang ups" because they affect the relationships he seeks to establish with his clients. Such exploration is equally important in the helping profession of teaching but, in the past, has seldom been included in the typical teachers' college curriculum.

SOME RESEARCH-BASED PURPOSES OF EFFECTIVE TEACHERS

Some of the research reported in earlier chapters on which this book is based attempted to study some of the purposes of good and poor teachers. Results seem to indicate that good professional workers perceive in common ways about themselves and others. Research has also demonstrated that good professional workers can be discriminated from poor ones on the basis of purposes in at least two other professions. The purposes of effective counselors, for example, have been found to be:

1. Self-revealing rather than self-concealing.
2. "Freeing" rather than "controlling."
3. Altruistic rather than narcissistic.
4. Concerned with larger goals rather than smaller ones.[2]

Similarly, effective Episcopal priests were found to have purposes described as freeing rather than controlling; becoming involved rather than avoiding involvement.[3]

Recent research has also shown that effective teaching is, in part, the product of certain kinds of purposes. Good and poor teachers, for example, can be distinguished with respect to the following kinds of purposes.[4]

1. Good teachers perceive their purpose in teaching as being one of freeing, rather than controlling, students. That is to say, the teacher perceives the purpose of the helping task as one of freeing, assisting, releasing, facilitating,

rather than as a matter of controlling, manipulating, coercing, blocking, or inhibiting behavior.

2. Good teachers tend to be more concerned with larger rather than smaller issues. They tend to view events in a broad rather than a narrow perspective. They are concerned with the broad connotations of events, with larger, more extensive implications, rather than with the immediate and specific. They are not exclusively concerned with details but can perceive beyond the immediate to the future.
3. Good teachers are more likely to be self-revealing than self-concealing. They are willing to disclose self. They can treat their feelings and shortcomings as important and significant rather than hiding or covering them up. They seem willing to be themselves.
4. Good teachers tend to be personally involved rather than alienated. The teacher sees his appropriate role as one of commitment to the helping process, a willingness to enter into interaction, as opposed to being inert or remaining aloof or remote from action.
5. Good teachers are concerned with furthering processes rather than achieving goals. They seem to see their appropriate role as one of encouraging and facilitating the process of search and discovery as opposed to promoting or working for a personal goal or a preconceived solution.

Other characteristics with respect to teachers' purposes have been suggested as connected with good teaching but have not yet been subjected to research.[5] Good teachers' purposes are those of

1. Helping rather than dominating.
2. Understanding, rather than condemning.
3. Accepting rather than rejecting.
4. Valuing integrity rather than violating integrity.
5. Being positive rather than negative.
6. Being open rather than closed to experience.
7. Being tolerant of ambiguity rather than intolerant.

All the characteristics of effective helpers indicated in the research mentioned above are broad categories of purposes. Within each of these there is room for the individual to find his own more specific ones. If such purposes are truly characteristic of the helping professions, as these researches seem to suggest, they also provide us with important clues as to what needs to be done in the teacher-education program. Somehow we shall have to find ways of involving our students in active consideration of their own and society's purposes.

SOME LIMITS OF FORMAL COURSES FOR DISCOVERING PURPOSE

Most teacher-education programs recognize the importance of a study of purposes, and they include this study in their programs in courses with such titles as the Philosophy of Education, School and Society, the Social Foundations of Education, and the American School. Unhappily, these courses have often failed to accomplish their objectives in anything like the degree we had hoped. The teacher who has not been exposed to classes designed to teach him about democracy in the course of his professional preparation would be rare indeed. Nevertheless, the failure of teachers to understand and apply the principles of democracy in the classroom is the despair of teacher-educators everywhere. It is apparent that the mere exposure of people to ideas is by no means a guarantee that they will espouse them.

At least three factors have important bearings on the failure of formal courses to fulfill our hopes in the discovery of purpose:

1. *The Attempt to "Give" Students Purposes.* As we have seen in Chapter 3, there is a vast difference between knowing and behaving. Abstract ideas do not affect behavior until the individual has discovered their personal meaning for him. This principle is nowhere more important than in the problem of the teaching of purposes.

The typical course attempts to provide the student with concepts usually provided in an orderly systematic fashion dictated by the logic of the subject matter. This arrangement puts the cart before the horse for learning does not proceed in orderly fashion. Order is imposed on what is learned after the learning has occured. Structure and meaning follow experience. They are not given to students; they are discovered by them. Until the student has entered into a kind of interaction with subject matter and has discovered a personal meaning in it, even his teaching field is a flat, meaningless thing, lifeless and antiseptic. It is form without essence. It cannot even be communicated except in a rigid, self-defeating fashion.

Recognizing that the provision of subject matter alone is insufficient to guarantee learning, Bruner and others have advocated the organization of content to emphasize principles, generalizations, and theories rather than isolated facts.[6] Unfortunately, such an organization is still not enough, for meaning lies, not in the subject matter, but in the learner. Emphasizing structure organizes information and makes more available the essence of the discipline studied, but it still represents only the information phase of learning. The discovery of meaning must still occur in the student.

2. *The Seduction of Language.* The principles of philosophy, sociology, and anthropology are concepts extracted from experience and formulated for handy use in dealing with further experience. The attempt to teach such concepts in the absence of experience forces both teacher and student to deal with these matters in purely verbal terms. Instead of developing a personal philosophy, students and teachers are seduced into examining philosophies at arm's length. Words and concepts become important for themselves. Each of the social sciences has developed a court language of its own, like the ancient knight's "language of chivalry" to be used in jousting and tournaments. There is a prestigious "in-group" quality to such language, and it is easy for students and professors to be carried away by it. Higher education is overwhelmingly verbal, and having fun with words is one of the delights of the teaching profession. Unhappily, this may sometimes be carried so far that the ability to speak the language with elegance may come to take the place of learning.

3. *The Course Organization of Content.* The typical course, it should be understood, is an arrangement to satisfy the need of the instructor, not the need of the student. As a consequence much of education is, indeed, "providing students with answers to problems they don't have yet." The matter is particularly critical with respect to the discovery of purpose. The compartmentalization of knowledge is contrary to what the teacher-education program should be attempting to do. The understanding of society's purposes and the development of one's own system of beliefs are not matters to be formally taught for three hours' credit. The attempt to do so only contributes further to the student's feeling that what he learns in class has little or nothing to do with the practice of his profession.

The course organization of content may have been appropriate to the goals of the liberal arts college from which it was adopted. It is not appropriate for the teacher-preparation program charged with the holistic task of professional training. The social and philosophical purposes of education do not occur in neat sequential fashion. Quite the contrary. The problems students discover in the classroom are likely to involve every aspect of professional work—subject matter, methods, philosophy, purpose, social structure, administration, and human growth and development—not separately but simultaneously. To meet such needs our traditional structure will simply not do. It will be necessary for us to develop problem-solving programs in which students can explore whatever is needed as it is needed on the one hand, and to provide instructors skilled in helping them do this across the whole spectrum of professional work on the other.

THE PROBLEMS APPROACH TO DISCOVERING PURPOSES

The creative process of evolving a set of clearly defined, defensible educational purposes is frequently arduous, sometimes agonizing, and always exciting. That the process is sometimes painful and frustrating is readily apparent when we observe that, among other things, it involves the surfacing of and coming to grips with deeply imbedded belief and attitudinal systems. That is, the aspiring teacher must identify clearly what he thinks is worthy and in what order of priority. For most of us, these belief and attitudinal components creep into our bloodstreams as if by osmosis. Few of us have taken the time or made the effort to identify and acknowledge these well-entrenched beliefs and attitudes. While it is undoubtedly painful to "know thyself," it is imperative that aspiring teachers engage in the process. Taking stock of self is a prime requirement for the creation of a defensible, respectable set of educational purposes. Purposes lie inside individuals and cannot be given to them. The teacher-preparation program can only provide the opportunities and conditions in which purposes can be explored and their personal meanings discovered. To do this effectively we must apply the same conditions for learning that we have already advocated for exploring the self in the previous chapter. We must seek continual involvement of students in activities that will spur them to question purposes and goals and that provide opportunities for the students to explore and think about them. Learning will come about as a consequence of the students' finding personal answers to such questions as

1. What is really important?
2. What am I trying to do?
3. What do school and society want of me?
4. What do I really want out of teaching?
5. Is what I want worthwhile?
6. Are the things I am doing fulfilling my purposes?
7. Are there better, more important, purposes that I might turn my attention to?
8. Whose purposes are most important here?

It is probable that some variation of the problems approach to teaching is most likely to result in the kind of personal discovery required for the development of effective teachers. Instead of presenting the student with the principles of the topic and asking him to apply them to himself as the usual course organization does, the problems approach tries to help the student extract the principles from his own experience or as a consequence of confrontation with important problems. It attempts to challenge and stimulate students to ask new questions and acquire new knowledge. It involves the student simultaneously in new experiences and in active consideration of their meaning both for himself and for the society of which he is a part.

The problems approach calls for involving the student in all the ways we suggested in Chapter 3. It asks him not simply to get his feet wet in the profession, but to immerse himself in the problems, practices, and ideas of teaching in every way he can. At the same time, the program is designed to encourage and assist him in exploring and discovering the meaning of all this through contemplation of his experiences. It attempts to keep him continuously engaged in an alternation of practice and exploration, of getting into predicaments and figuring how to get out of them, of watching and thinking, of trying and talking, of making mistakes and trying again. Out of this kind of confrontation with problems and the continuous search for Why? What for? What is good? What works? What is important? What do I believe?, purposes and principles become formulated in ways that can later be counted on to make a difference in how the teacher behaves.

A New Organization of Subject Matter

One of the things almost certain to happen as a result of the problems approach to the teaching of purposes will be the disappearance of psychology, sociology, philosophy, and anthropology as separate and distinct subject areas during the early phases of the professional program. This need not disturb us. There is plenty of time for students to tackle the formal disciplines of these subjects if they wish to do so later. Beginning students need experience before organization and system can be meaningful. A college student is often but a beginner in many areas of experience despite his adult appearance. "Advanced-ness" is not a question of age or year in college. It is a matter of experience with problems. Most beginning teachers are no more ready to examine the formal aspects of philosophy, sociology, anthropology, or psychology than the fourth-grade child is to deal with the theory of grammar or the beauties of topological mathematics. These subjects only become separate matters in abstract study. In life situations they are inextricably intertwined. They are experienced simultaneously but formally studied individually. There is already under way a movement to place formal courses in these subjects at the graduate level; this move seems a good one. Philosophy, sociology, psychology, and anthropology should be an integral part of *all* the student's learning experiences during his professional preparation.

There is another reason why we need not be unduly disturbed at the intermingling of the various academic disciplines. Increasingly we are coming to recognize that each of the social sciences is but a different way of looking at the same problem—the nature and behavior of human beings. On some campuses there is even a strong movement to combine these groups into single departments of "human relations." This move is often resisted by professors fearful of losing their identity, but despite opposition the idea continues to find increasing favor.

The organization of subject matter at elementary levels around student need will also require a change in thinking about faculty competence and the recognition that highly specialized knowledge is not necessarily required for good teaching at such levels. This will not be easy in most colleges because it runs head-on into rigid job descriptions by which most faculties are chosen. Once established, these job descriptions are jealously guarded even when they no longer have relevance or meaning. Job descriptions assume that human talent is entirely organized around content or "knowledge of the subject."

One finds everywhere hundreds of articles written on the role of the teacher, or counselor, or principal, or visiting teacher, or school psychologist, and so on, as though these roles could really be defined by prescriptions instead of by people and their behavior. The assumption that beginning teachers can only be taught philosophy, psychology, sociology, aesthetics, or curriculum by experts in these fields is simply not true without reference to the level at which the problems are to be confronted. Roles defined in terms of content are only valid if content is the only question with which we are concerned.

Beginning students need to get acquainted with problems and to explore where these problems may take them. This calls for a kind of instructor who may not be a content specialist but, like the elementary teacher, an expert in encouraging and assisting the processes of learning. Teaming such persons with the content experts would provide both information and exploration aspects needed for the problems approach. A number of colleges have already been experimenting with procedures of this sort with excellent results. Among these are the University of Florida;[7] San Francisco State College;[8] the Project I studies at Rochester, Cornell, Buffalo, and Syracuse universities,[9] University of Massachusetts, Colorado State University, and the State University of New York at New Paltz. All of them attempt to involve students deeply in professional matters and each has experimented with various ways of providing students with rich experiences in content as well as opportunities to explore and discover its meaning in seminars or discussion groups under the supervision of leaders.

ENDNOTES

[1]Charles Silberman, *Crisis in the Classroom* (New York: Random House, 1970), p. 36.

[2]A. W. Combs and D. W. Soper, "Perceptual Organization of Effective Counselors," *J. Counsel. Psych.* 10, no. 3 (1963): 222–226.

[3]John A. Benton, "Perceptual Characteristics of Episcopal Pastors," Unpublished Ed.D. Dissertation (Gainesville: University of Florida, 1964).

[4]C. T. Gooding, "An Observational Analysis of the Perceptual Organization of Effective Teachers," Unpublished Ed.D. Dissertation (Gainesville: University of Florida, 1964).

[5]A. W. Combs, "The Personal Approach to Good Teaching," *Ed. Leadership* 21 (1964): 369–378.

[6]Jerome S. Bruner, *The Process of Education* (New York: Random House, 1960).

[7]I. J. Gordon et al., "The Florida Experiment in Undergraduate Teacher Education," in *Changes in Teacher Education* (Washington, D.C.: National Commission on Teacher Education and Professional Standards, N.E.A., 1963).

[8]F. T. Wilhelms and A. E. Siemons, "A Curriculum for Personal and Professional Development," in *Changes in Teacher Education* (Washington, D.C.: National Commission on Teacher Education and Professional Standards, N.E.A., 1963).

[9]W. L. Irvine, "Project I: An Experimental Program for the Preparation of Secondary School Teachers," in *Changes in Teacher Education* (Washington, D.C.: National Commission on Teacher Education and Professional Standards, N.E.A., 1963).

8

The Personal Discovery of Ways to Teach

As we have seen in the early chapters of this book, the search for methods of teaching that are "good" or "right" for all teachers is fruitless. Modern psychology tells us that methods are but ways of accomplishing purposes. They are vehicles for achieving results. Whether their effects on others are good or bad depends on who is running the vehicle, what he is trying to do, and how this is perceived by those he is doing it to. This personal approach to the problem of methods helps us to understand why so much of our former "logical" approaches to teaching did not produce the results we so earnestly hoped for. Looking at methods in this way, one may see new directions for attention and experimentation that hold promise for more efficient production of the kinds of teachers we so desperately need.

Part of our former difficulty in respect to teaching techniques came about because we tried to find "general" methods, ways of operating that would get results "across the board." Many educators still do. They keep hoping for methods that will work in all times and places and for every variety of teacher. They gather round some methods like political party banners and will fight to the death for team teaching, phonics, behavior modification, performance-based teaching, or the particular fad that happens to be in vogue at the time. But skill in teaching, as we now know, is not a mechanical matter of using the right methods at the right time. It is a creative act involving the effective use of one's self-as-instrument. Preparing teachers is not a question of teaching them "how." It is a matter of helping each to discover his own best ways. We do not mean to say that one method is as good as another or that any method one uses which gets results is appropriate. On the contrary, we are saying that the choice of methods is one of the very important ways in which the teacher uses himself as an instrument. The problem is not, What is the right method? but What is the most *appropriate* method to fit the individual teacher's personal perceptions of the following?

1. The nature and content of his subject.
2. What he believes his students are like.
3. How he sees himself.
4. His own and society's purposes.
5. His understanding of the nature of the learning process.

If there were but a single factor to be taken into consideration under each of the five headings above, the task of finding the "right" methods appropriate to these categories would be within the realm of possibility. But within each of these categories there may be hundreds of variations, and the chances of finding the right methods become astronomical. Even the behaviors we call "habits," which most of us are used to thinking of as repetitions of an action, are now described by psychologists as never being done the same twice. Each human behavior is a creative act, a complex response of a person to the situation he sees himself to be in. So it is with methods. Each teacher must find his own best ways of teaching. This will require continuous seeking and experimentation throughout his professional career.

To make this discovery most effectively, student teachers need

1. Many rich opportunities for involvement with students and with teaching.
2. Concurrent opportunities to plan for such experiences and to discover the meanings of them after they have occurred.
3. An atmosphere that actively encourages and facilitates self involvement and personal discovery.

A FACILITATING, ENCOURAGING ATMOSPHERE

The Importance of Feeling Safe

For most people there is a natural reluctance to giving self over to untried and unknown circumstances. When one is committed, one can be hurt. Many young people have been sufficiently humiliated in their previous experiences both in and out of school to make them approach with caution new situations that hold a potential for further self-damage. They have a real need to play things safe, but the discovery of methods requires of the student that he risk himself. As we have already seen in our discussion of the atmosphere for learning, such exploration is most likely to take place when the individual feels safe and secure. Only the foolhardy take risks that are not likely to pay off. It is important, then, that a warm, friendly, understanding, and encouraging atmosphere characterize all aspects of the student's exploration of methods. Every effort must be expended to make his experiences as challenging and unthreatening as possible. Students should be given major responsibility for their own learning, encouraged to "stick their necks out" in all kinds of experimentation, and dare to get involved to the very limits of their capacities. If this is to happen, however, it will require a high-grade staff of sympathetic people, able to provide support and assistance when needed and skilled in protecting students from humiliation, embarrassment, and failure.

Since it is the student's self that must be fashioned into an effective instrument, the atmosphere for personal exploration must begin with an acceptance of the self the student brings with him. It is the function of professional education to produce changes in the self, to be sure. There is a world of difference, however, in a program that begins by giving the student a feeling that his self as it stands is enough for now and can be helped to become adequate, or a program that diminishes and degrades the self by continual harping on its insufficiencies. Acceptance of self, as any psychotherapist is aware, is essential to personality change. One can only progress from where he is. He cannot start from where he is not. So it is necessary that professional students begin with the feeling, "It is all right to be me," and "This self with which I begin can become a good teacher."

The atmosphere we seek involves accepting each student's self as it is, including his preconceived notions about teaching. Instead of rejecting these out of hand, they are taken as the place where this student begins and are accepted, considered, discussed, tried, tested, and modified by his own experience. Each person's own beliefs about teaching serve as his point of departure.

The principle of readiness, which governs so much of what teachers do in their daily jobs, must also be applied to the teacher's own experience in learning to teach. Student teachers need to explore and try out what they are ready to do. The methods with which they experiment need to be those with which they can feel comfortable and with which they have a chance of success. No matter how clever or sophisticated a method may be, its value to the student is dependent on whether it *works for him*. The things that will *not* work for a given personality are so many that it does not really pay to explore them. The precious time available to help a student become a teacher is much better spent on things that fit than things that do not.

It is important, also, that the consideration of methods be approached in relaxed fashion. It is not necessary that all possible ways be considered or tried or even thought much about. Too much pressure to make a choice, especially if it must be the "right" one, may have the effect of impeding any choice whatever. Who has not had the experience of walking into a bookstore or record store and being so swamped with the thousands of choices available that he walked out again without buying anything, or worse still, with a purchase he did not really want? The opportunity to try a few is much more likely to be helpful than standing immobilized before a thousand, unable to make a choice. Record and bookshop clerks have learned from experience that the browsing customer is more likely to buy than the hurried one. The same principle seems true when applied to shopping for methods.

Eliminating Barriers

To bring about an atmosphere conducive to the personal exploration and discovery of techniques, instructors need to root out barriers that lie in the path of such exploration. It goes without saying that a program oriented about helping the individual find himself has no room for invidious comparisons or competition among students. Learning to be a teacher is a developmental task of increasing uniqueness. As with an artist, we cannot compare his pictures with others. We look at the changes occurring from picture to picture of one artist and value each artist for his difference from others.

The failure of students to understand the personal character of methods may create an additional barrier. Most beginning students share the commonly held conception that there are "right" methods of teaching. This belief may seriously interfere with the very learning we hope to produce. When methods are stressed, the student's attention is directed to the wrong place for solving his problems. When methods are practiced, it is methods that are the center of attention, rather than the goals of teaching. Psychologists point out that only one thing can be in the center of attention at one time. With attention centered on method or procedure, the teacher cannot properly respond to the individual needs of students with whom he is woking or to changing conditions in the classroom that call for changing techniques. It is even possible that preoccupation with specific techniques may seriously interfere with the student's success as a teacher by concentrating his attention on the wrong questions.

There is a little rhyme:

The centipede was happy quite
Until a toad in fun
Said, "Pray, which leg goes after which?"
That worked her mind to such a pitch
She lay distracted in a ditch,
Considering how to run![1]

So it is with teaching: Over-concern with method may get in the way of the smooth operation characteristic of good teaching.

Good teachers do not agonize about their methods. They have discovered ways of teaching that serve their purposes, and they move easily from one to another with their minds focused on the children and their problems. "Sally is afraid she will fail if she tries. Ben is feeling insignificant and left out of the activity right now. Eddie must have a task that is more challenging." The competent teacher does *what needs to be done* once he has perceived the problem, and he does it almost automatically.

The teacher who worries "Am I doing this the right way?" or "Will someone think what I am doing is not what I should be doing?" cannot be properly tuned in to the problems of Sally, Ben, or Eddie. Instead he is tuned in to his own problem, and he will miss the clues he needs to be aware of in order to respond appropriately. Student teachers can easily become trapped in such cycles of worrying about the correctness of their methods, failing to perceive the real problems of children, responding to their own need to do things the right way, and so responding inappropriately to children.

The other-directed teacher, able to act only on the direction of superiors, is often seen in schools today. He is usually a person filled with anxieties who seeks approval from his fellow teachers or superiors through conforming behavior. This is hardly the model we want to encourage new teachers to emulate. If we continue our past mistakes, however, and convince young teachers that there is "a right way" to do things that we know and they must learn, the result will be the perpetuation of the mindless, other-directed teacher. To assure that this does not happen means we must give students and young teachers opportunity to think, to decide, and to act on the basis of their own values. In the process of doing so these values will become strengthened, and the teacher will become stronger and more decisive.

Misconceptions about Children and Learning

Common misconceptions about children may often create additional barriers to exploring techniques. One of these is the belief that children are basically evil, the natural enemies of adults. With such a feeling about his pupils the beginning teacher can hardly afford to do much experimenting with methods. Seeing children on the other side of every question, he is likely to be so busy hanging onto his power and authority that he does not risk trying anything new. It often comes as a great surprise to student teachers that children can be trusted, that most of them are not scheming to embarrass or destroy their teachers. Some experienced teachers never get over this fear, even after fifty years of service. The fact is, however, that children, like everyone else, want to be adequate. They *want* to learn if they can be freed to do so. They really want the same things their teachers do for them—to grow up to be worthwhile, important people.

Another misconception has to do with children's fragility. They are often assumed to be delicate and likely to be irreparably harmed by any single thing a teacher may do. This notion has been fostered by some psychologists' stress on the traumatic events in a child's life. The consequence of such emphasis on trauma has been to make many parents and teachers afraid of children. It is interesting to see how many teachers who fear doing something that will destroy a child at the same time will hold an equally firm, but inconsistent, belief that the child is entirely the product of his parents and what teachers do does not matter! Actually, what teachers do does matter, but not so much that any one event is likely to destroy a youngster. Children are tough and can take a great deal. If they could not, they would never grow to adulthood.

There are other misconceptions about children and learning that stand in the way of accurate understanding. One of these is the notion that children will not learn unless "motivated" to do so by marks or grades. In spite of the fact that thousands of children have gone to schools that did not give grades and achieved as well as those who did, this belief lingers on.

Another misconception concerns the storing of information for use at a future time. "They should realize that even if they do not need to know this material right now they will one of these days," is a commonly heard excuse for teaching irrelevant facts to children. All of us have had the experience of learning something, only to forget it after the course ended, and later when the knowledge was really needed it was no longer there. We waste a great deal of time and effort this way, and, in the process, convince many children that school deals only with things that are unimportant.

Some teachers have these misconceptions mixed up in their minds with more valid beliefs, but because they are not sure of what they believe they are easily misled by slogans and popular stereotyped ideas. For example, a teacher may hold with equal conviction the following beliefs:

1. Children are naturally lazy and must be "motivated" by someone else before they will learn.
2. Children are essentially good.
3. The child's self-concept is of the utmost importance in his reaction to school.
4. For their own good, children must be forced, if necessary, to learn the fundamentals of communication and quantification (3 R's).

Such a teacher, while believing that children are "good," does not trust them to be self-motivated. He wants to enhance the self-concept of the child, but he is willing to use force to bring about learning. This teacher is confused, and, until he finds out what he believes, he will have difficulty choosing appropriate methods. He will have to decide whether it is more important to enhance self-concepts of children or force learning on children when they do not want it. It is impossible to have it both ways.

Freedom to Experiment

Finally, it is essential that the atmosphere for exploring methods be one that values and encourages experimentation. It must give students the feeling that mistakes are of minor consequence and the really important thing is trying. Whatever gets in the way of the freest possible opportunities to experiment—even with the wildest, most far-out notions—should be eliminated. Students who are afraid to experiment fall back on the methods used on them. This is not so bad when those methods fit, but the attempt to adopt someone else's methods when they do not fit can be disastrous.

When students are afraid to try, they rely on crutches of one sort or another, like the age-old advice to beginning teachers, "Start out tough! Don't let them get away with a thing! You can ease up once you have them under control." Unhappily, once having come to rely on such crutches, some students are never able to give them up. The future of the profession is dependent on teachers who are deeply ingrained with the experimental attitude. This attitude should begin with the very first teaching experiences.

PERSONAL INVOLVEMENT WITH STUDENTS AND TEACHING

For a very long time our teacher-education programs have operated on a philosophy of "preparing to teach." Students were taught the "good" methods or "right" methods with the expectation that after they had learned them well, they would then apply them, first in student teaching and then on the job. For most students this meant little or no contact with live children until the day they entered the classroom for their student teaching experience. Student teaching was regarded as a kind of examination at the *end* of learning rather than a learning experience in itself. This is a dreadful waste of a wonderful opportunity.

Participation in teaching should be the occasion of learning, not of testing methods after learning is finished. Young teachers ought to be involved with students and teaching at every step of their professional development. The laboratory for the student teacher is interaction with people in all kinds of settings and particularly in educational ones. Long ago we learned that the gradual approach to teaching children to swim or breaking horses to the saddle was superior to throwing them in the water or riding the bronco down. In similar fashion the learning of methods needs to be a slow process of discovering solutions to problems and one's own best ways of working. This calls for continuous opportunities to be involved in teaching activities rather than a single traumatic plunge at the end of the professional program. Ideally, this kind of program would begin with students "helping" teachers at the very outset of their professional work with the time and responsibilities involved smoothly increasing throughout the period of professional education.

Each teacher-education curriculum can give different kinds of opportunities for involvement, depending on local conditions. Some programs make full use of these opportunities, but others are not even aware of what resources exist in the local area, beyond those officially established for student teaching or internship experiences. A great deal more imagination needs to be devoted to searching out and contriving involvement experiences for all students in every phase of their education and at every level of participation, whether it be observation, or working with single individuals, with small groups, or with large classes.

In recent years we have come to appreciate the importance of early involvement for quite another reason. Increasing technology and industrial automation has created a world that demands more and more knowledge and skill of all our citizens in order that they will be able to pull their proper weight.

We have also launched a national effort to eliminate poverty, and we are looking to our public schools for ways of helping persons from every class of our social system to achieve the maximum of which they are capable. These are bold and exciting goals. Whether we achieve them will depend very largely on our success in educating teachers to work effectively with the most needy of our citizens.

This calls for teachers who are ready and able to get out of their familiar ruts and confront aspects of the world they did not know existed. In the past we have characteristically drawn our teachers from the middle class. Many of them do not know what it is to be poor, or hungry, or rejected, or subjected to minority group pressures like discrimination. Yet many of these teachers will find their first positions working with just such people. We cannot afford to prepare them to teach in a world that does not exist. To help them discover their own best ways of teaching, they need to be immersed in educational and human problems just as deeply as they can take it, with the security and help of friendly persons around them to help when the going gets rough and to provide encouragement and assistance as it is needed.

The Personal Approach to Supervision

The self-as-instrument concept of good teaching calls for a new conception of the role of supervisors in the education of future teachers. The task of supervisors is usually conceived as one of helping students learn how to teach. Often such instructors are chosen because they are master teachers able to teach extremely well. This very expertness can get in the way of helping teacher-education students to discover their own best ways of teaching. The supervisor's task must be to help another person find *his* best ways of teaching. Lindsey comments on this point:

> Being a master teacher does not, by itself, qualify one for leadership in the field of teacher education. To work with the prospective teacher as a colleague in guiding learners

> calls for special competence, no small element of which is the ability to teach "through" another person. Many a master teacher finds it very difficult, if not impossible, to share his skills with a novice, to recognize and appreciate ways of guiding learning other than his own, to safeguard the interests of learners, while at the same time giving the teacher-to-be, freedom to "try his wings."[2]

The master teacher who conceives of his job as a matter of helping the student learn to teach as he himself does will defeat the very purposes of teacher education as we have outlined them in this book.

Conant suggests the use of "clinical professors" as supervisors of student teachers. These are persons "prepared by training to understand what other specialists have to say, and inclined to listen to them, and prepared by continuing experience in the elementary or secondary school to demonstrate in concrete teaching situations the implications of expert judgment."[3] There seems much merit in this suggestion. Supervisors who do not themselves engage in front-line activities can all too easily slip into the trap of teaching students *about* teaching rather than helping them find their own appropriate ways of teaching. Indeed, this error is so easy to make that even active involvement in teaching will not of itself insure escape from it.

It is a rather frustrating experience to ask a good teacher about his methods because he often cannot tell you about them. Since he rarely thinks about methods, questioning him about them is very likely to be embarrassing because he probably believes he *should* know good reasons for his behavior. Consequently, he will make up some for you that will almost certainly be *only parts* of the real reasons. Let us take an example of a good teacher whom we have observed doing "just the right thing" with a child. She behaved the way she did because, among other things, of the ways she saw him, how she saw herself, how she saw the problem the child faced, how it looked from his point of view (empathy), how she saw the rest of the class, how she was feeling, how she felt the child was feeling, where they were in the lesson, where they were in the hour, how far along this child had come in his studies, what he is ready for and what is too much for him, and so on. Impressed with what she did, we ask her, "Miss Brown, why did you do that?" The answer we get is not at all why she did that. She tells us why she thinks she *must* have done that! What we get is a psychologist's explanation of the historic reasons bearing on the problem, the child's performance, past history, what he needs, *some* of which had a bearing on what she did, to be sure, but which are only a pale excuse for the warmth, color, vitality, and sparkle of the real thing. A preoccupation with what teachers do may only serve to point the student's attention to the wrong places for change and destroy the effectiveness of the supervisor as well.

Focusing on Causes Rather than Results

Formerly, we have conceived the task of the supervisor as a "critic teacher," someone who would assist the student to evaluate his performance and find new and better things to do. Emphasis was on the teaching act, what the teacher did. The effect of this concern with the student's behavior, however, is to focus attention on results rather than causes. As modern psychology tells us, behavior is only a symptom of internal states of feeling, seeing, believing, and understanding. To help people change behavior, it is on these factors we must concentrate. This calls for a shift in the basic orientation of supervisors. Instead of focusing attention on what students *do*, they must learn to concentrate on how student teachers feel, think, believe—about themselves, their students, their purposes, and the subject matter they are charged with teaching.

Supervisors in many other fields have learned they are more likely to get results by bypassing the question of methods to deal with the more important questions of the student's beliefs, feelings, and understandings. The counselor-educator, for example, explores with the student such questions as: "How do you feel about your client?" "How do you suppose he feels about that?" "What is it you are trying to do in the time you have with your client?" The supervisor sees his role not as one of teaching methods and techniques, but of helping the student counselor to explore his own perceptions and beliefs about the critical questions that govern his behavior. Supervisors in teacher education must learn to be concerned with similar problems.

To help students in this way calls for supervisors who are more than master teachers. They must also be skillful in establishing warm, nonthreatening relationships with student teachers and must possess clear understanding of what is needed to be truly helpful in assisting students to explore and discover their own best ways of operation. This calls for supervisors whose own thinking about what is important and what constitutes good teaching is clear and enlightened. They will also need to be people capable of much self-discipline so that they do not make the mistake of imposing their own values on those whom they are supervising. In addition to being knowledgeable in their own right, persons chosen for these kinds of responsibilities will need to be people with respect for the dignity and integrity of others, who will value difference, and who are able to respect the right of student teachers to find their own best ways.

THE USE OF DISCUSSION GROUPS FOR EXPLORATION OF PURPOSES

The use of discussion groups has become an increasingly popular method of instruction in many teacher-preparation programs. In some it is even used almost exclusively while other methods are regarded with much disdain by the faculty. There is no doubt that well-run discussion groups can provide valuable experiences for students. The interaction involved in such groups lends itself especially well to the exploration and clarification of personal purposes. Like any other method of teaching, however, groups are no panacea. What students get out of them varies greatly. They can be exciting and fruitful or downright dull and banal, depending very largely on the skill of the leaders.

Some of the failures of discussion groups to live up to expectations seem to be due to a confusion between two different kinds of discussion groups. Each of these has important values, which unfortunately are often dissipated or destroyed by otherwise skillful instructors who are not aware of the differences between these two kinds of groups and so use them inappropriately.

The Decision Group

One approach to group discussion might be called the "decision group." Here the purpose is to explore a problem and arrive at a kind of decision about it. In the course of acting in the decision group, members may learn a great deal about the problem under observation. This group is also a kind of small-scale model of what our democratic government is like. As a consequence, such groups are popular with instructors concerned about "educating for democracy."

As a means of helping members discuss issues and arrive at group decisions, the decision group has immense value. As a technique for inducing learning and the exploration of purposes, however, it has some serious limitations. The decision group is focused on group action, and its goal is arriving at a decision. But learning is an individual matter, and this objective may actually impede effective learning.

The moment a group is required to come to a decision, it begins to operate in ways that coerce its members. It tends, therefore, to cut short individual exploration and discovery in favor of arriving at a group decision. In a decision group there inevitably comes a time when the members who have arrived at a decision begin to put pressure on those who have not. This coercion may be applied with great gentleness so that people are not even conscious of what is happening to them. One way to clothe the iron hand with a velvet glove is to call for a vote. Despite the general acceptance of the vote as a veritable symbol of democracy, it is nevertheless a coercive device of great power, especially on those in the minority. As one of our students expressed it, "A vote is only a means of stopping a discussion." People can be forced to participate, but involvement is another matter requiring an act of will on the part of the person. There is an important place for the decision group in education, but as a technique for inducing effective learning it leaves something to be desired.

The Learning Group

The second type of group we call the "learning group." Its purpose is to allow members to explore and discover ideas and their personal meanings. Since the exploration and discovery of meaning is a purely personal goal, there is no need in such a group for a group decision and, hence, no coercion of individual members. It is even conceivable that there might be less agreement at the end of the discussion than at the beginning. The atmosphere in a learning group is one of mutual assistance and interaction in a setting in which the dignity and integrity of individuals are respected.

To help students in our classes at the University of Florida use such groups more effectively, we have devised a set of suggestions describing learning groups and how to get the most out of them. We include it here as a thumbnail description of learning groups for interested readers.

GROUP-DISCUSSION SUGGESTIONS

What Is a Group Discussion?

It is easy for a group of people to engage in talk, but this does not mean that they are having a group discussion. A group discussion is not a debate. Neither is it a bull session. The purpose of a debate is to convince other people of the rightness of one's own position. "Convincing" may even proceed without any real regard for accuracy, but only with a desire to win the argument irrespective of the merits of the position. A bull session, on the other hand, is a pleasant sort of pastime in which one seeks to regale others by descriptions or stories of things he knows or events which have happened to him. Bull sessions are a kind of friendly game of "one-upmanship" in which one person tells a story and the next seeks to top it with still another. Good group discussions are neither of these. The purpose of group discussion is neither to win an argument nor to amuse oneself. Its purpose is to explore and discover personal meanings.

There are two kinds of group discussions in general use in teaching. One of these is the decision group in which the primary purpose is to arrive at a consensus or decision on a matter. Almost everyone is familiar with such groups and has participated in them at one time or another. Decision groups can be very helpful in bringing about an agreement on a plan of action. Unfortunately, they may also interfere with the freedom of the individual to explore and move in directions unique to his own needs for decision groups have the unhappy effect of coercing their members to arrive at the approved solutions.

A second type of discussion group is the "exploratory" or "learning" group. In these sessions the purpose is not to arrive at decisions, but it is to help each member explore ideas and discover meanings through interaction with other people. Much of our everyday talk is made up of description in which we seek in one way or another to convey ideas to other people. It is usually concerned with what we know. It proceeds with such expressions as "I saw," "I said," "He told me," "There was," etc. A learning group discussion is far more tentative, even halting, in its progress for it deals not with certainty but with search. It is an exploration of feelings, beliefs, doubts, fears, and concerns. Listening to a group discussion, one is likely to hear such expressions as "It seems to me," "I'm not sure about this but," "Sometimes I wonder if," "What do you think about?," "I think," "I believe," "I wish," and even sometimes if a group feels very safe with each other, "I'm afraid," "I'm angry about," or "I love." Group discussion does not seek to convince. Rather, it deals with matters unsolved and seeks to help each member find meanings not existing before.

A good group discussion is not brought about simply by bringing a group of people together to talk. Good groups take time to form, and it is only as the members of a group discover each other as warm, friendly people over a period of time that good group discussion can come about. The following are some suggestions that may help you to make your group a more profitable one for all concerned.

General Considerations

1. For good thinking there must be a sense of relaxation. Group discussion should always be leisurely, not desultory or wandering, but also not hastened or tense. It is more important to think slowly and thoroughly than to cover any prearranged amount of material.
2. Although we hope that all members of our group will feel free to contribute to the discussion and will want to share their thinking with others, we also recognize that for some people this is a difficult and trying thing to do. No one in our groups is under compulsion to speak. Participation is not measured by words spoken, and a silent person may be participating more than his more verbal colleagues.
3. The purpose of the group discussion is the discovery of personal meaning. This calls for "kicking ideas around," testing them, "trying them on for size," examining, comparing, and thinking about and talking about ideas until they fit the particular needs and being of each person. This is best accomplished when group members are willing to express their own thinking, beliefs, and feelings freely on the one hand and to listen receptively and sympathetically to other people's ideas.
4. Sometimes in a group discussion there may be periods of silence. These need not cause concern. They are a normal function of group discussion which occur at points when a group is thinking deeply, is in process of shifting gears, or has exhausted a particular question.
5. Group discussion proceeds best in an atmosphere of warmth and friendliness. Nothing causes people to clam up quicker than being threatened, ridiculed, or humiliated. An atmosphere of acceptance and an honest seeking for understanding is most conducive to good group operation. The more quickly you can get to know and appreciate your fellow group members as individual

people, the more quickly your group will begin to pay dividends in growth and development of its members.

Some Specific Suggestions to Group Members

1. Maintain an attitude of searching for a solution. You are trying to find the best answer, not trying to convince other people. Try not to let your previously held ideas interfere with your freedom of thinking. Be on guard against the effect of your own prejudices. You will find this difficult but highly rewarding.
2. Speak whenever you feel moved to do so (and have the right of way, of course) even though your idea may seem incomplete. If the answers were all known, there would be no point in exploring.
3. Cultivate the art of careful listening. You can practice this by trying to formulate in your own mind the gist of what a previous speaker has been saying before adding your own contribution.
4. Try to stay with the group. Discussion that strays too far afield may kill the topic at hand. Avoid introducing new issues until the decks are clean of the business under discussion.
5. Talk briefly. Saying too much may cause people's minds to wander so that they miss the value of what you wish to express.
6. Avoid long stories, anecdotes, or case studies that only illustrate a point. It is ideas, beliefs, implications, and understandings that are the meat of a discussion. Listening to one person after another tell long tales of "what happened to me" can quickly destroy a good discussion.
7. Be as sympathetic and understanding of other people's views as you can. If you disagree, say so, but avoid the appearance of being belligerent or threatening other people.

Ground Rules for Our Discussions

1. Cross-examination of other speakers is not permitted. Remember that a group discussion is netiher a debate nor

a trial. The object is to explore one's own thinking in interaction with others, so we have made it a rule that group members may not ask questions of other group members that smack of cross-questioning or that might prove embarrassing. When you feel the urge to cross-question another, try instead expressing what you believe and inviting comment and criticism about that. (Make positive statements and take responsibility for them. "I feel . . ." or "I believe . . ." is better than "Don't you think that . . .")

2. Traffic rules. Speak whenever you feel moved to do so without seeking recognition as long as the track is clear. However, whenever the traffic gets heavy and more than one person seeks to speak at once, then look to the leader to direct the traffic and seek recognition before speaking.
3. A group discussion can only operate well when all members are concerned with the issues before the house. We have therefore made a rule to restrict side conversations to a minimum. Do not hold lengthy conversations with your neighbors as this forms new groups and destroys the cohesiveness of the total group. Besides, it is not very well mannered.

THE CURRICULUM LABORATORY

The self-as-instrument concept of professional work that we have advocated in this book requires helping the student find and use the very best methods of teaching that will suit him. Teaching methods is a question of helping students explore and discover purposes, techniques, self, and subject matter. These must be encountered as a whole, not in unrelated bits and pieces, as the discovery of methods is not a matter of putting things together in the most logical form. Rather, it is a question of finding those techniques that best fit a unique individual operating in a complex and changing set of circumstances. We believe this calls for a laboratory approach to the question—a workshop type of operation.

What is needed is not courses in methods, but curriculum laboratories—places where curriculum materials are available in abundance and where students can explore and try out all kinds of equipment, supplies, and materials. Such laboratories may operate in close conjunction with libraries, but they should also provide space for experimenting with materials needed by teachers in carrying out their jobs. They should also be available when students need them, open at all times so that students can browse as they wish or work by themselves or with others. There should even be opportunity, if the student wishes, to set up materials and leave them for a period of time while he continues to experiment with them. Some medical colleges now provide small offices within the college assigned to medical students. Working in their own offices, students can get the feel of professional work in a professional setting. Perhaps the day may come when we will regard similar facilities as important aspects in the education of teachers as well.

Education students need to be surrounded with rich opportunities to see the kinds of methods and materials other people have found useful. This can be provided by observing teachers in action, by opportunities to examine curriculum materials through reading, demonstrations, and the whole gamut of media devices now available to us. It is important, however, that the student be given opportunities to explore these materials at his own speed and in terms of his own needs and without prejudice. The moment that labels of "good" or "bad," "right" or "wrong," become attached to methods and materials, students are no longer free to explore at will. The pressure to be on the "right" side restricts choices. Worse still, if he has the misfortune to be seduced into trying a method that does not fit him, he may reject the method forever because "it doesn't work" when the real difficulty was that he wasn't ready. The student subjected to many such experiences may even end with the conclusion that his instructors "don't know what they are talking about," that "educational theory won't work," or that "this progressive education jazz is 'for the birds.' "

An attitude of critical appraisal should reign in the laboratory in order to avoid either blanket acceptance or rejection of methods. There *are* things that can be taught very well by lectures, television, teaching machines, and the like. There are also things that cannot. To deal with all methods as dichotomies—as though they were good or bad—only compounds the problem and makes it less likely that we will find adequate solutions. Good teachers cannot afford either to go overboard for a method on the one hand or to resist what it honestly can do on the other.

The kind of laboratories we have pleaded for in the paragraphs above, in which students can be free to experiment in whatever ways they choose, will provide important opportunities for students to interact with each other, to see what others are doing, to involve themselves in argument and discussion, and to test ideas in the open marketplace. Additional opportunities for this kind of exploration can be provided in the various kinds of demonstration and group-discussion activities provided by the college as a part of its regular curriculum. We have already discussed some of these group activities.

The supervisor or teacher of the kind of laboratory we have been describing will himself have to be a first-class teacher with a wide variety of skills, sensitivity to the needs of students, and an enthusiastic willingness to share himself and his skills with student teachers. The kinds of teaching he does should be demonstrations in action of the best he knows about teaching so that students not only talk about teaching techniques but experience them as well. What is more, the supervisor should be sufficiently secure so that he can permit, and even encourage, students to critically examine his methods and procedures without fear of reprisal. It takes real understanding on the part of supervisors to let students be and to set aside their own pet methods and ideas while helping a beginner find his. All things need to be open to discussion in the curriculum laboratory, including the supervisor himself.

In the search for personal techniques for teaching, there should be no unreal distinctions between what is good for public schools and colleges. Teacher-preparation programs are often criticized because some of the things taught, particularly in classes preparing elementary teachers, seem a far cry from traditional college procedures. Education students learning children's games, learning how to make papier-mâché figures or number boards for teaching arithmetic, or gathering files of useful materials are sometimes disdainfully regarded by nonprofessional students as engaging in "Mickey Mouse" activities. But every profession has its simple techniques as well as its profound and scholarly aspects, and one is no good without the other. Such criticism should not dissuade the teacher-preparation programs from engaging in whatever is necessary for the production of teachers. Whatever is useful and helpful, no matter how simple or bizarre, should find its proper place in the curriculum laboratory, as long as it contributes to the exploration and discovery of useful techniques for the students involved.

EVALUATING TEACHING METHODS

A major problem in education is the endless parade of fads and panaceas that teachers confront as they go about their work. New commercial products to assist the learning process come on the market every day. New methods are proposed almost as frequently. It is important that teachers choose wisely which of these new products and ideas they will adopt for use in their own classrooms. This choice rests on the teacher's ability to evaluate methods of teaching according to his own teaching values.

Three considerations are most important in the selection of methods of teaching. They are

1. The effectiveness of the method.
2. The effect of the method on its user.
3. The effect of the method on the recipient—the learner.

If a method were not more effective than its alternatives there would be no reason to consider using it. The first question to be asked then is: *Does the proposed method produce better learning, or require less time, effort, or material resources?*

Assuming a positive answer to the first question, we must then ask, *What is the effect of this method on the user?* Does it interfere or improve his relationships with his class? Does he feel better about himself as a result of using this method? Does the method tend to narrow his thinking or make him a more closed person?

If the answer to the second question is positive we then ask the third, *What is the effect on the recipient?* How does the learner feel when this method is used? Does he feel more able and satisfied? Does he feel closer to the teacher and his classmates? Does he have a desire to continue learning? Are there any negative effects on the learner?

For example, a teacher might consider using a new method for the teaching of reading that relies heavily on materials found in the child's environment such as newspapers, food containers, comic books, TV advertising, etc. Since the cost of materials will be lower than it would be for a set of reading books, if the amount and quality of learning is at least as high as it has been with the more traditional materials, the teacher is justified in thinking that the first test has been passed.

To carry the example further, suppose this method calls for children helping each other to a greater extent than the method the teacher had been using. If the teacher perceives the situation as an opportunity to spend more of his time with individual children who need the teacher's expertise he will feel good about what is happening to him, his view of the teaching-learning process will be broadened, and he will be more open to new ideas in the future.

Finally, if the children in our example feel more involved in the process of their own learning, if they feel success, greater trust, and identification with the teacher and with their classmates, the last hurdle has been jumped and the teacher can justifiably judge the method a success.

We could just as easily have given negative answers to the evaluation questions in this example. Suppose the children did not learn as much or as fast. There would be no point in asking the effects on the user and the recipients. But even if the learning results were positive, if the effect on the user were to make him feel less useful, or to cause him to see the learning process in narrow, mechanical terms, we would conclude that this method is potentially disastrous. In the long run both children and the teacher will suffer because of it.

By the same token, if the effect on the children were perceiving the teacher as rejecting them or the establishment in the group of a caste system (those who *can* set apart from those who *cannot*), the method would be a failure, *even if the children had learned more reading.*

Selecting methods of teaching is a complex task calling for the most sophisticated kind of thinking on the teacher's part. As difficult as it is to do, and as imprecise as the evaluation process is, the job is one that cannot be delegated to anyone other than the teacher who works with the particular children in question on a continuous basis. Those who occupy the ivory towers can help teachers *think* about methods. Those who occupy administrative offices can help by providing access to materials and in-service education, but only the classroom teacher can make the decision as to which methods to employ with his students.

ENDNOTES

[1]Mrs. Edward Craster in *Pinafore Poems* (1871).

[2]Margaret Lindsey, *New Horizons for the Teaching Profession* (Washington, D.C.: National Commission on Teacher Education and Professional Standards, N.E.A., 1961).

[3]J. B. Conant, *The Education of American Teachers* (New York: McGraw-Hill, 1963).

9

Organizing the Professional Aspects of a Teacher-Preparation Program

So far in this book we have been exploring the bases for an effective teacher-education program from current knowledge about learning and behavior change. But how would one go about constructing one? What would it look like? At the present time there is no existing curriculum that incorporates all the elements about which we have been speaking. What is more, it is unlikely that any one program ever will. Teacher-education programs, like teachers themselves, need to serve local needs and purposes. There will probably be very few opportunities to build new programs from scratch. We shall have to be content with encouraging institutions to examine assumptions, eliminate local barriers to change, and push forward wherever possible to new ways of educating teachers.

The purpose of this chapter is to suggest what a teacher-education program, congruent with our foregoing observations, might look like. Our major concern is that of proposing the broad theoretical framework for such a program. To put some warm flesh on these theoretical bones, our points will also be illustrated by referring to an existing elementary teacher-education program at the University of Florida.

The New Elementary Program (NEP) began operating in the winter of 1969 as an experimental program side by side with the prior existing program, and in the fall of 1972 it was approved by the university as the regular program for all students majoring in Childhood Education. The program was designed in 1968–69 to implement many of the principles discussed in this book. The original group of 60 students expanded to 120 during the first year and a half, and that number has become established as the size of an NEP team.

In the fall of 1972 the second team of NEP was begun, and the third started operation in the winter of 1973. The NEP designation was changed to CEP (Childhood Education Program) when the program dropped its experimental status. By the fall of 1973 the fourth and final team was operational. Each of the four teams will function independently from the others, but the basic assumptions about teacher education that we have outlined above will serve as a starting point for all of them.

PROFESSIONAL ASPECTS OF A TEACHER-EDUCATION PROGRAM: THE INADEQUACY OF ORGANIZATION AROUND CONTENT

A curriculum primarily concerned with content lends itself to a neat hierarchical organization in which materials can be presented step by step in sequential order. Various prerequisite arrangements can be established to control the entrance of students to courses. This is the traditional pattern of course offerings existing in the typical liberal arts college department of mathematics, biology, chemistry, and the like. It is also the organization taken over years ago by most teacher-preparation programs for their own use. Unfortunately, it is most inadequate for our modern purposes.

A sequential structure of courses makes some sense when content is the essential matter to be dealt with. Professional education, however, is not a discipline in its own right. It represents the application of a number of other disciplines. As we pointed out earlier in Chapter 6, professional education has different purposes and goals than do the liberal arts. We cannot be satisfied with "knowledge about" child development, methods of teaching, curriculum, etc. Instead, teacher education must help students integrate their knowledge with their developing values concerning education and children, with their own self-concerns, and with their experiences with children and schools. All of this must contribute to an emerging belief in themselves as effective instruments for the education of youth.

The inadequacies of the old content organization become even more glaring in the light of the concepts of learning and of good teaching on which this book is based. Learning conceived as the acquisition of content means that the individual can be continuously presented with new material as rapidly as he can assimilate it. Learning as behavior change calls for the discovery of personal meaning. Professional preparation requires a deeper grasp of basic principles as well as the acquisition of new data.

It is necessary, therefore, to organize our efforts around the learner's needs rather than the subject matter. When an education student feels the need to know about effective methods of reading instruction, for example, he will learn the concepts involved very quickly if the material is available to him. He also may need to reexamine some ideas a second, third, or fourth time in order to develop a deeper, more personal understanding of their implications. It is a basic principle of learning that people learn more effectively when they have a need to know. It follows then that the presentation of material and the opportunity to examine and reexamine it must come as a result of the *student's felt need,* not the need of the instructor to cover the subject matter. As the student engages in this process of becoming aware of his own need to know, expressing that need, acting on it, and learning relevant concepts as a result, he senses a growing belief about himself that he is able and that he is becoming an increasingly effective instrument with which to achieve his purposes. This growing self-concept as teacher, coupled with the increased understanding, which is its major component, leads to the desire for more learning. Teacher-education programs must be organized in such a way that students can seek information when they need it, seek the same information more than once, if need be, and be provided information when it seems relevant to their lives.

THE NEED FOR FLEXIBILITY

A professional program built upon the self-as-instrument concept must break out of old traditions that sought to provide *common* experiences. Maximum flexibility is called for. To provide this kind of flexibility we will first have to shake ourselves loose from the lockstep of some of our traditional ways of organization. The familiar concepts of courses, credit hours, classroom scheduling, grading practices, examinations, and the like may often be helpful in organizing learning around content. They may also seriously interfere with producing a change in *people and their behavior.*

An efficient program must

1. Permit the movement of students at different speeds.
2. Provide content and experience in response to student needs.
3. Provide simultaneous, rather than sequential, experiences for the learner.
4. Place much more responsibility on the student himself.

The professional program must provide opportunities for students to progress at varying rates of speed. Anything less is wasteful and inefficient. We advocate increased flexibility in public education so that children may move at their optimum rates. Can we, in good faith, do less for our education students? The good teacher is not a finished product, but a human process. This process may be observed at various stages of development, but it is never complete or finished. People come to us at various levels and move at varying rates of speed. The teacher-education curriculum does not *produce* teachers. It would be more correct to say that it "begins" them. It enters the life of the individual for a short period, helps him orient himself, and turns him loose on his own once again. This means the adequate program must be prepared to pick the student up at whatever point he has reached on entrance and carry him forward as far as possible in the time he is with us. This is not easy, but it is possible.

The adequate professional program will also be geared to student needs. There is little point in teaching what the student cannot grasp or what he already knows. These are principles that everyone in education knows and with which they agree. Yet throughout the teaching profession there is probably no principle more often violated. It is so much more convenient to handle students as though they were alike, even when we know they are different. If, however, we are to make any headway in helping teachers apply what is known about individual differences in their classrooms, we must show them good examples in their own education. Where else but in their own experience can this be more appropriately demonstrated?

The concept of the good teacher we have been talking about calls for a simultaneous, rather than a consecutive, order of experience. The perceptual aspects of the good teacher that we described earlier do not take place one after the other, but simultaneously. As one changes his views about the nature of people, he also changes his conceptions of his relationship to them. Such changes in turn have their implications for the ways in which the individual perceives his purposes and procedures. Methods, too, will change with changes in the individual's ways of perceiving himself, his world, and his task. The self of the teacher is an interdependent organization, not a series of isolated boxes that can be dealt with one at a time.

If the person of the teacher is seen as the center of the problem of teacher education, the organization of teacher-education programs around subject matter and methods is simply no longer tenable. The definition of the good teacher we have been talking about does not lend itself to this kind of neat packaging. A problem-oriented, personal-growth-oriented program flows over all boundaries.

For the program we envisage, it will be necessary to place much more responsibility for learning on the student himself. We shall have to trust students more. We shall have to grant them a larger responsibility for their own education than some colleges have been willing heretofore to contemplate. Responsibility is the very essence of the professional worker. Responsibility, however, is learned from being given responsibility. It is never learned by having it withheld. A program of professional education must treat its students as responsible people and encourage the growth of responsibility through independent action on the part of students. To achieve such a goal the teacher-education curriculum will need to give very careful attention to at least three major principles.

1. It will need to expect and demand that its students take an active part in their own education. Students must be treated as responsible, independent, mature persons. From the beginning of their professional education they must be treated as professional people, able to make decisions and accountable for their consequences.
2. It will need to involve students intimately in the planning and direction of their educational experiences and programs. This seems essential for the kind of responsibility we seek. Students must be given a voice in matters that concern them and opportunities to consider and plan for further experiences. A program built around student needs which does not involve students in the business of its own planning seems an anomaly indeed.

3. The college will need to provide the administrative, instructional, and physical facilities for encouraging individual and small-group communication and experimentation in every way possible. The faculty and its administrative staff will need to examine their facilities with an eye to eliminating the barriers to interaction and personal involvement, on the one hand, and actively seek to encourage involvement, on the other. It must be recognized, too, that barriers to student interaction and communication are by no means all physical. Administrative rules and regulations, originally conceived to facilitate the achievement of certain purposes, have a way of developing an autonomy of their own and continuing to exist long after the purposes they were meant to facilitate have changed to something else.

BASIC ASSUMPTIONS CONCERNING HUMANISTIC TEACHER EDUCATION[1]

Dr. Robert Blume, in an article entitled "Humanizing Teacher Education," has stated a series of assumptions which he believes are basic to teacher education. They provide a useful summary of many of the discussions we have been carrying on throughout this volume and seem to the authors to provide valuable guidelines for the designing of a humanistic teacher-education program:

1. People do only what they would rather do (from Freud). That is, people behave according to choices they make from among alternatives they see available to them at the moment.

2. Learning has two aspects: (1) acquiring new information, and (2) discovering the *personal meaning* of that information. Information itself is useless. Only when individuals find the link between specific information and their own lives are they able to put it to use. This principle is not well understood by educators. Most of our efforts to improve education involve new ways to deliver information to people. Very few innovations

involve helping learners to discover the personal meaning of that information.

3. It is more appropriate for people to learn a few concepts rather than many facts.

4. Learning is much more efficient if the learner first feels a need to know that which is to be learned. This principle has been known for a long time, but the response of educators to it has been to artificially "motivate" students with letter grades and other rewards. None of these schemes works as well as the genuine desire to learn, and in fact they frequently get in the way of that desire by substituting artificial for real motivation.

5. No one specific item of information, and no specific skill is essential for effective teaching. Any one fact or skill that could be mentioned might be missing in a very effective teacher. Furthermore, it would be presumptuous for teacher educators in the 1970's, drawing on their experience in the 40's, 50's, and 60's, to declare certain teaching skills or knowledge essential for teachers in the 80's, and 90's, and beyond. We just don't know what the job of the teacher will be in 20 years, or even 10. Hopefully it will be quite different from what it is today.

6. People learn more easily and rapidly if they help make the important decisions about their learning.

7. People learn and grow more quickly if they aren't afraid to make mistakes. They can be creative only if they can risk making errors.

8. Objectivity is a valuable asset for a researcher, but it is not very useful for workers in the helping professions, such as teaching. What is needed instead is the opposite of objectivity—concern and caring. As Jack Frymier has said, we want students not only to know about cold, hard facts, but to have some "hot feelings about hard facts." We must produce teachers who have developed strong values about teaching.[2]

9. Teachers teach the way they have been taught—not the way they have been taught to teach. If we want elementary and secondary teachers to be warm, friendly people who relate positively and openly with their students, then we must treat them that way in our college programs. We must respect our teacher-education students if we expect them to respect their pupils.

10. Pressure on students produces negative behaviors, such as cheating, avoidance, fearfulness, and psychosomatic illness. Students tend to become more closed in their interpersonal relationships when they are pressured.

11. Our teachers would be more effective if they were self-actualizers. Teachers ideally should be more healthy than "normal" people. They should be creative, self-motivated, well liked persons.

THEORY INTO PRACTICE

Teacher education is undergoing great ferment today, and it is clear that the old order is changing in fundamental ways. Not all of the changes, however, are in the direction suggested by this book. Some are attempting to train students in specific skills in the hope that these skills will be retained and used by teachers, after graduation, in their own classrooms. This approach is part of a *closed system*, which assumes prior knowledge of the desired end point of the process and is geared to produce precisely that product. A number of colleges of education, for example, are working on extensive lists of behavioral objectives that they will require all students to achieve. The assumption behind this scheme is that by learning many "competencies," or bits of information, one will emerge with *general competence*. We do not accept this assumption, but believe rather that competence grows more effectively out of deep understanding of the processes of growth and development and experience with children in real teaching-learning situations.

The *open system* we have in mind assumes only that the general direction of desired growth is evident beforehand, and as a student becomes more and more a teacher he will have more to say about the kind of teacher he wants to be. As he increasingly discovers the personal meaning of the information and experiences with which he comes into contact, he redefines his goals in ways which are relevant to his growing understanding of teaching. To illustrate the way in which such an approach might be implemented, we include here a description of a program in which the authors have been intimately involved. (See Figure 9-1.)

This program, originally called the New Elementary Program, at this writing (fall 1973) has graduated approximately 200 elementary teachers. Students are engaged in three broad categories of experience throughout the approximately two years they spend in the program: involvement with children, exposure to ideas, and the discovery of personal meaning, generally referred to as (1) field experience, (2) substantive panel, and (3) seminar.

The Provision of Practical Experience

Traditionally, the aspiring teacher's practical preparation has been isolated into a few weeks of teaching experience variously labeled "practice teaching," "teaching internship," and the like. Usually, such an experience is tacked onto the backside of the professional program on the assumption that students should learn how to teach, then go try it—a procedure that has shown great lack of success to date. Our theoretical persuasion—confirmed by several years of implementation—convinces us that a radically different approach to practical experience is called for.

Instead of limiting the prospective teacher's field experience to a practice episode which comes at the tail end, it makes more sense to make it a *continuous, integral* part of the *entire* program. In this way field experience becomes, not only an opportunity to try things already mastered, but an experience to find out what the problems are and what yet needs to be learned. This continuous, practical involvement is graduated increasingly both in terms of time spent and responsibility assumed. The beginning student is assigned to work with a single child in a one-to-one relationship. This may be a tutoring situation or a nonschool setting such as a day care center or boys' club. At the same time the student visits the laboratory school to observe children at various levels.

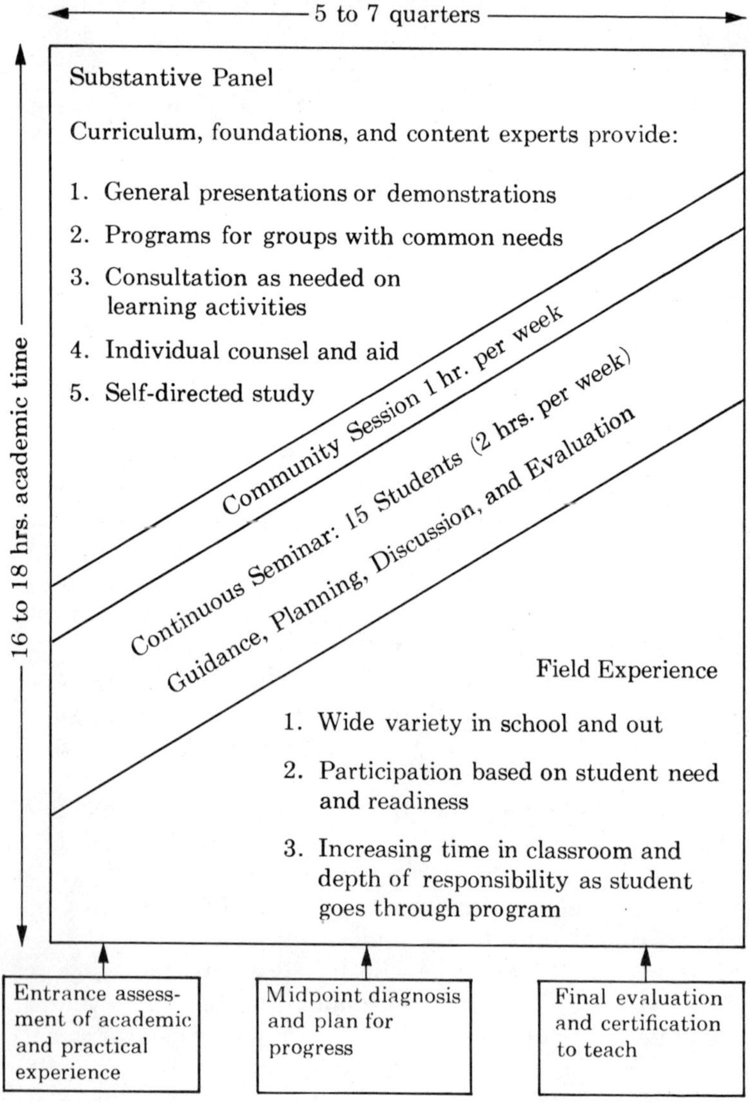

FIGURE 9-1. College of Education—University of Florida Schematic Diagram: New Elementary Program, Junior—Senior Years

The next level of field experience requires serving as a teacher aide in an elementary classroom. Following this he takes on more responsibility for the planning of learning experiences as an "assistant teacher," followed by experience as "associate teacher" involving still more responsibility. Finally, after at least four quarters of such experience he takes over completely the role of teacher for his last half-quarter in the program. This graduated process of teaching involvement is paced differently for every prospective teacher consistent with what he is ready for. When he should shift gears is determined after open discussion among the student, his seminar, and public school and college personnel with whom he has worked.

A crucial feature of the type of field experience provided by the New Elementary Program is that prospective teachers should experience different types of teaching approaches, i.e., open classroom, self-contained classroom, team teaching, modular teaching, etc. Of equal importance, it should provide opportunity for the young teacher to interact with varied types of students, i.e., students from varying economic, ethnic, cultural, urban, or rural backgrounds. The teacher-to-be should also have the opportunity to interact with youngsters of different age levels so that a student, initially convinced that he wishes to teach at a given grade level, may change his mind and decide he is more comfortable with youngsters of greater or lesser maturity.

A typical field experience configuration, drawn from hundreds of such examples in the New Elementary Program files, might read as follows:

Student Z: *Weeks 1–10:* Observed ten times in multi-age classes at school A (a rather modern, well-equipped campus school where flexible, open teaching occurred).

Weeks 1–10: Tutored a youngster at the same school.

Weeks 11–19: Teacher initiate on second-grade level at school B (a well-equipped suburban school in an affluent part of the city where the student was exposed to a self-contained classroom taught by a rather authoritarian teacher).

Weeks 20–30: Assistant teacher on sixth-grade level at school C (a rather poorly-equipped school located in an inner-city ghetto area in which an open classroom, similar to the English Primary School approach, was in operation).
Weeks 31–40: Assistant teacher at school D on the second-grade level (a "prestigious" school located in a well-entrenched middle-class neighborhood where the teacher adopted a rather inconsistent eclectic approach).
Weeks 41–50: Associate teacher at school C in a third-grade classroom in a rural community twenty miles from campus.
Weeks 51–60: Student interns at school C (takes complete charge of same third-grade classroom).

Field experience ought not to reside exclusively in the classroom, however. Rather, it should include student involvement which is *community-wide* in scope. The student's perceptual field will be enriched by experiencing a wide range of differing community experiences. Such opportunities are endless—an evening's participation in a school-sponsored bazaar; attending church services; playing pool with youngsters at the local Boys' Club; and sitting in on an occasional school board meeting are just a few examples. Only as the classroom teacher becomes acutely sensitive to the mores of the community in which he or she will be employed can rapport and empathy be established.

In such ways the NEP attempts to use field experiences as a vehicle in which each student:

1. Will confront real problems and a wide variety of children, teachers, and teaching strategies.
2. Can discover his own strengths and weaknesses and develop further needs to know.
3. Can try his wings in settings paced to his current capacities to cope. It is important that teacher-educators provide not only theory but a means for the student to observe and participate in the process of turning the theory into practice. Such extensive, continuous field experience, we have found, is also one of the ways teacher

education can provide the relevancy students have been clamoring for in recent years.

The Exposure to Ideas

The second type of experience provided for students is designed to make maximally available the resources of the community and the faculty for exposing students to ideas. This involves a wide variety of experiences aimed at providing information, stimulating thinking, airing controversies, confronting students with professional problems, demonstrating methods and techniques, or giving students opportunities to see and hear persons with important things to say for educational thought and practice. Some of these sessions are required of all students. Some are established in response to the needs of particular groups. Others are simply made available to students without requirements of any kind. Some experiences provided in this phase of the students' preparation are planned long in advance; others are set up on comparatively short notice. To assure that all students and staff members are informed as to resources available, a calendar of events is provided and revised weekly. Using this calendar, the student and his adviser can determine between them which events the student will be *required* to attend, which he might *choose* to attend, and which he could safely ignore.

The University of Florida's New Elementary Program was patterned after these suggested guidelines. The main opportunity for students to experience a range of differing ideas and attitudes is provided by the Substantive Panel. This panel, staffed by regular faculty, makes available learning experiences in various areas of inquiry, such as language arts and math education. Several features distinguish this substantive experience from most traditional approaches:

1. Professors work with students in a different way. They begin each term by announcing a series of orientation meetings for those students who have not begun that particular area of study. In these meetings the panel member

explains how students can proceed to study in the area, what is required for its completion, and some of the salient points of the area itself. Thereafter, the professor holds small-group meetings, which students may attend at their option, in which lectures and demonstrations are given, discussions are held, and questions are answered. Professors also schedule sufficient office hours to work with students individually on projects and independent studies and encourage students to work together in cooperative ways on some learning activities.

2. The content of a substantive area is organized around a series of "learning activities" (LA's) some of which are required of all students, some are selected by the student from alternatives, and some are proposed by the student and approved by the instructor. The latter are called "negotiated activities," and require students, either independently or in small-study groups, to present a contract spelling out what they intend to do and how it will be done. The following is a typical Learning Activity Description sheet in the area of science:

New Elementary Program
University of Florida

Lynn Oberlin
Fall 1972

Science Learning Activities

Complete six of the following. The first four are required. Orientation sessions are a prerequisite to other activities.

*1. Attend Science Orientation Sessions and demonstrate competence in science content. (Science content module available.

*2. Learn to use the Science Teacher Observation Rating Form (STORF) and demonstrate competence observing two taped situations. As a member of a three-person team, observe (with the STORF) at least two science lessons being taught and teach at least one lesson which is observed (with the STORF) by two team members.

*3. Learn about new programs in elementary school science (AAAS, ESS, SCIS). Examine and perform the activities for six units. This must include at least two of the programs.

*4. Develop plans and materials, and use four of the following techniques in teaching science to children: a. Science Center Component, b. Counterintuitive (Discrepant Events), c. Pictorial Riddles, d. Open-ended Investigation, e. Inductive Teaching.

5. Select and carry out two laboratory investigations in each of the following areas: a. Physical Science, b. Life Science, c. Earth Science. (Three different sources are required.)

6. Present evidence that scientific information has been learned in two areas of physical science and two areas of biological science. Two sources of adult material must be used for each area. (Areas must be narrow in scope.)

7. Demonstrate an understanding of the "Processes of Science." (Module available.)

8. Plan and teach a science UNIT (several lessons) to children. The following must be provided for: Active involvement of children, differing achievement and ability levels of children, general student planning, student choices, student planned inquiry, use of manipulative materials.

9. Teach a UNIT (several lessons) of one of the new programs (AAAS, SCIS, ESS) to children. Learning Activity #3 is a prerequisite.

10. Evaluate two state adopted textbook series at three consecutive levels. All series must be evaluated at the same levels.

11. Propose other learning activities that will help the student to become a better teacher of science in the elementary school.

*Required

The above activities may be amended or changed completely through student-instructor agreement.

After attending the orientation sessions in a given area a student is free to pursue his study in that area as he sees fit. He may pace his work in the area according to his needs, interests, and opportunities. For example, he may find that he knows nothing about teaching science although he would like to introduce his children to some ideas about pollution. Upon examining the bulletin board he may find that the science instructor will hold a series of small-group meetings on that topic so he may sign up and participate in the associated activities, such as readings and laboratory work at the same time.

On the other hand, it may be that the science instructor has just completed such a group and does not plan to offer it again for two more quarters. In this case the student might (1) pursue this topic independently, according to the prescribed learning activity, or (2) find a friend or two who would also like to work on it with him, (3) get some other students to join him in a request to have it repeated sooner, or (4) contract to do a special study in this area. If the latter course is chosen it would be natural to apply the associated planning to his work with the children in the field, in his contractual responsibilities. He would thus be killing two birds with one stone: (1) he would be fulfilling his duties in the school to plan and carry out learning experiences with children, and (2) he would be satisfying one of the requirements in the science area. The important point is that the student is free to choose which alternative way he will carry out the activity.

3. There are no letter grades for the work in the NEP (only "satisfactory" and "unsatisfactory"). The student does not "fail" his learning activities in the traditional sense. Rather, he is invited to redo, or add to, those which the professor feels are less than adequate.
4. In many substantive areas, the student has the opportunity of arranging to do an in-depth project in lieu of several shorter LA's. For example, in Social Foundations of Education, there are six activities, three of which are required. The student who is genuinely enthusiastic about a given area of inquiry relevant to Social Foun-

dations—say the political socialization of the elementary child in a big city—can arrange with the professor to do an in-depth study of this process as a substitute for other LA's he wishes to omit.

5. Integral parts of most substantive areas are the small-group discussions. These are casual experiences in which students and faculty together discuss various concepts, issues, and problems. The purposes of these groups vary. Some function to clear up obscurities and confusions. Others are established to discuss in depth the relationship between given LA's and actual classroom observations. Others—frequently initiated by students—are set up to explore areas (oftentimes only indirectly related to the completion of specific LA's themselves) to which a group of students is "tuned in" and "turned on." For example, while Social Foundations of Education has no required LA's in Women's Liberation or the Education of the American Indian, both topics have been excitingly explored. In both instances, the discussions were the product of student initiative. Another interesting aspect of some of these small-group discussions is that they are sometimes instructed by the students themselves. For example, a very articulate young lady, deeply into Women's Liberation, conducted a six-week seminar, from which her male professor learned a lot!

The Discovery of Personal Meaning—The Seminar

"Home base" for students in this program is a group of thirty students and one faculty member, who form themselves into a small community of persons seeking to learn and to help each other learn. These thirty are divided each term into two discussion groups which meet weekly for two class periods. The primary purpose of these groups is for each student to discover his own personal meanings through exploration of himself and the ideas and experiences he has been exposed to in the previous week in an atmosphere designed to further such exploration and discovery.

Students are assigned to an ongoing seminar when they enter the program, filling a vacancy left by a recent graduate.

The group thus consists of students at various stages of their development. This system makes it possible for "older" students to help "younger" ones. In the process of answering questions raised by younger students the older ones reexamine their own thinking and refine their values; they become more aware of, and committed to, their ideas of teaching and learning.

Forward-looking elementary educators have been aware for some time of the fact that children learn as much, or more, from other children as they do from their teachers. This principle is certainly evident in teacher education, where we deal with young adults who search for answers to real problems wherever they may be found, and the professor's "expert authority" must be earned rather than conferred. The seminar uses this principle to its advantage by legitimizing student-to-student teaching and learning. In the process, professors learn a great deal about what is happening in today's schools, as well as what is happening in the heads of the students.

Another important purpose of the seminar is to provide an atmosphere of interest and concern for each member of the group, thus giving him the emotional support he needs to risk thinking about new ideas. (It is important to note here that competitive grading has no place in this program. More information about the evaluation process will be given later.)

The activities in the seminar range from discussions of field experiences to communications labs and social gatherings. Values clarification games are sometimes played, and students hear reports from the Program Meeting, where both faculty and students gather to make policy decisions about the program. The seminars sometimes divide into triads or dyads for discussion purposes, and they occasionally meet with another seminar group for a social gathering.

The seminar leader serves as the personal counselor and academic adviser for each student in his seminar for the duration of his time in the program. In cooperation with the students he keeps all the records on their progress and carries out the overall evaluation functions. The friendly, long-term relationship between student and seminar leader makes it possible for the student to talk about his problems and worries in an open way. He is also able to hear the feedback from his seminar leader much more clearly because of the lack of threat involved in the relationship.

Seminars meet in a variety of places such as classrooms, faculty homes, and student apartments. Ideally, comfortable seminar rooms would be available on campus for such purposes. Informality is important for the creation of a warm, friendly atmosphere. This may mean sitting on the floor, kicking off one's shoes if one wishes, drinking a coke, and relaxing with close friends. Sometimes music and television are assets to the seminar. The members of a seminar might watch a network program on drug education, for example. Unfortunately, such facilities are not available on our campus and seminars, therefore, many times meet in off-campus locations rather than classrooms.

The length of time students spend in the program varies with the individual, generally between four and seven quarters. This variability seems strange to some educators; since needs of students are variable programs must also be. The decision about how long a student will spend in the program is made by the seminar leader in consultation with the student and other faculty members.

PROBLEMS OF ORGANIZATION AND ADMINISTRATION

The first reaction on looking at a program that departs so widely from many existing procedures may be to throw up one's hands in despair at the administrative problems involved. However, whether or not such a program is administratively convenient ought not determine whether the effort is made. Acceptance or rejection of an unorthodox program should be based on more valid reasons than expediency. The critical question must be, Does it produce better teachers?

The typical college "faculty load" is determined by setting an arbitrary number of courses or credit hours for which each professor will be responsible. In the NEP substitute role responsibilities are substituted for courses. For example, the role of seminar leader is equivalent to one course; the role of science instructor is equivalent to one course; etc. The program is organized into teams of 120 students, 1 program director, 4 seminar leaders, and 1 substantive panel member for each area of study (art, curriculum, language arts, mathematics, reading, science, social studies, human growth and development, social foundations, multi-ethnic studies, music, health, physical education, and children's literature). These 18 responsibilities are sometimes handled by 10 or 12 professors because some faculty members may carry dual responsibilities. The more members of the faculty team double up on their responsibilities the smaller the team can be, and the easier it is to meet, to communicate, and to agree on policies.

Record keeping in a program of this kind is different from that in traditional programs. It is necessary to know at any given time which students have completed what learning activities, which field experiences they have successfully completed, how many quarters they have been in the program, and when they plan to complete it. This information is the responsibility of the seminar leader and the students, using feedback from substantive panel members and teachers in the field.

Liaison with Schools

In the traditional program with student teaching occurring in a term near the end of the program, it is customary to assign a faculty member to supervise the student in the internship experience. In a program which places students in the schools *every* term this is impossible. We have found that it is also unnecessary so far as supervision per se is concerned. The teacher in the classroom is the professional in the best position to do that, and the seminar leader has ample opportunity to discuss with the student the meaning of the experience to him.

What is needed, however, is a liaison person who understands the program, who understands the schools, and who is skillful in facilitating communication between the two. A field-based program must have the utmost cooperation among all the people involved: the college faculty, the student, and the schools. In the experimental phase of our program we have relied on one faculty member to do this job as a part of his responsibility for interns in the traditional program. Currently we are beginning a new phase of the procedure in which the seminar leader will assign his students to teachers within a limited number of schools designated for use of his seminar.

Program Meetings

From the beginning of the program students have been involved in all phases of the decision-making processes. Each seminar sends one delegate to the bi-weekly Program Meeting. At this meeting problems are discussed, special requests by individual students are considered, and decisions are made regarding future directions for the overall program. Students are not mere observers but actual participants who vote along with the faculty members on all matters which come before the group. When students are involved in policy making decisions there is much better acceptance of them. Decisions made in this way are much more realistic because they are made with the input of all persons who will be affected by them, not by the faculty alone.

EVALUATION

Our understanding of the purpose of evaluation is to provide feedback for learners, teachers, and others who have a need for it, in order to help them make better decisions in the future. We see a necessity for evaluation with regard to (1) student progress in all the activities in which they are engaged, (2) effectiveness of faculty efforts, and (3) effectiveness of the program itself. The three are closely related, of course.

Student Evaluation

The work of students is evaluated by students themselves, substantive panel members, teachers in the schools, and seminar leaders. The latter coordinate the whole process. Keeping in mind the three basic elements of the program: field experience, substantive area studies, and seminar, here is how our student evaluation is carried out.

1. Seminar leaders establish a folder for each student which contains a program record form.
2. When students complete projects and learning activities in each substantive area they are given a slip stating this fact and signed by the faculty member involved. If work is not done to the satisfaction of the faculty member no slip is given, thus the slip itself denotes satisfactory work. This slip is filed in the student's folder and entered on his record form.
3. When an entire area is completed a brief statement concerning the general quality of work in that area accompanies the last slip the student receives and places in his file. The seminar leader marks the area "completed."
4. Teachers with whom the student works in the field mail in evaluation forms similar to a standard student teaching evaluation each quarter. They are placed in the student's folder.
5. During the third quarter in the program a "midpoint review conference" is held. This conference involves the student, the seminar leader, and one or two faculty members from the substantive panel. The group examines the student's record to date and discusses his field experiences. The student's plans for the remainder of the program are also discussed and suggestions are made concerning the appropriateness of his plans.
6. Each quarter the student submits a "quarter contract" to his seminar leader outlining his expected progress for the quarter. At the end of the quarter the seminar leader reviews with the student his actual progress during the quarter.
7. At the completion of the program the student arranges a "final review conference" similar to the midpoint review. The student is asked to explore his thoughts and

feelings about the teaching profession, about himself as a teacher, about the program he has just completed, and about his future plans. The seminar leader writes a letter summarizing the student's work (using the statements turned in by substantive panel members) and briefly describing the program. This letter becomes a part of the graduate's credentials in the placement office.

Faculty and Program Evaluation

The University of Florida systematically seeks student feedback concerning the teaching done by faculty members in all courses. Because this rating is predicated on the standard course format, however, it is not very appropriate for our program, and we therefore gather additional information from students concerning their perceptions of our work. Students fill out evaluation forms on each substantive panel member once during the year, and on their seminar leaders three times each year. They also evaluate the entire program three times each year.

In addition to these formal ratings, other less formal means are used to find out what students think about the NEP and its faculty. The seminar itself is relaxed and informal enough to free students to speak their minds. If a substantive panel member is perceived as unfair, the seminars will be filled with discussions of his misdeeds, and usually this happens in unison. While this may seem threatening to faculty members at first, it is actually evaluation at its best, because the feedback to the instructor involved is immediate. This rapid communication permits him to (1) defend himself to the students, if need be, or (2) alter his procedures. Where there is some difficulty, in most cases, the problem is a lack of communication between instructor and students.

ENDNOTES

[1]Reprinted by permission of *Phi Delta Kappan* from Robert A. Blume, "Humanizing Teacher Education," *Phi Delta Kappan* LII, no. 7 (March 1971).

[2]This is not to suggest that teachers can be totally nonobjective in their thinking. They must, of course, pay attention to objective research about

teaching, for example. But teachers and students are warm human beings and that fact cannot be ignored. It must be recognized and accepted as a crucial aspect of the teacher-pupil interaction. A good teacher will respond to a child on the basis of his relationship with him. In addition to his awareness of the objective data about a child's performance he will not deny his feelings about the child in favor of test scores, previous grades, IQ's, or other "objective" data.

10

Accountability and Teacher Education

In previous chapters we have outlined the essential ingredients of a teacher-education program suggested by research on the "helping professions" and the principles of perceptual psychology. The last chapter described a program currently operating at the University of Florida that is attempting to place such a plan in action. But how shall teacher-education programs be evaluated? Everything in education must be accountable and teacher-preparation programs are no exception. The critical question is just how do we judge the effectiveness of new teachers?

The prime objective of teacher education everywhere is to turn out teachers skillful in helping children learn. Ideally, then, we should go into the schools and find out how the students of our graduates are faring. Unhappily, the problems of this kind of assessment are very great. Teachers' college graduates have a way of scattering on graduation to all points of the compass and with each one teaching anywhere from 30 to 200 children a day the sheer logistics of such follow-up studies would impose a financial strain that few college budgets could absorb. Even if this were not so there would remain the problems of choosing appropriate pupil measures to use as criteria for judging teacher effectiveness. Standard achievement tests certainly would not do. It is no secret that the national achievement tests commonly used in our schools measure but a fraction of what children learn: for the most part low-order cognitive skills but little or none of complex problem-solving, creative thinking, or skills that involve affect as much as cognition. But even if adequate pupil measures existed, other problems would remain, for example, establishing whether a given child's gains or losses could truly be ascribed to the teacher one sought to assess. What, then, can we do to determine the effectiveness of a teacher-education program?

In this book we have described the effective teacher as one who has learned to use his self as an effective instrument to carry out his own and society's purposes: the self-as-instrument concept. Such a definition means that we cannot hope to find precise behaviors likely to apply to all good teachers. We have seen that there is literally no such thing as a "good" or "right" method of teaching that we can expect to find characteristic of good or bad teachers. Good teaching is an exercise in effective problem solving involving the intelligent use of all the resources at a teacher's command. It is a highly creative and personal activity. So much so, in fact, that the attempt to define "teacher acts" and apply them as yardsticks for the measurement of effective teaching must always remain an inadequate approach to assessment. Since teachers are unique and children are unique, any hope of finding universal descriptions of their behavioral interactions is useless before it begins.

BEHAVIORAL OBJECTIVES AND PERFORMANCE-BASED CRITERIA

It is currently fashionable to attempt the assessment of educational outcomes through the use of behavioral objectives and performance-based criteria. The procedure requires teachers and/or students to state the objectives of any learning situation in clear behavioral terms and to indicate what acts or performances will be acceptable as indicators of whether, indeed, objectives were adequately met. This approach to accountability seems so logical, straightforward, and business-like that it has been widely hailed as the key to making our educational efforts more effective at every level of operation including teacher education.

There can certainly be no doubt that the behavioral objectives approach is useful and valuable for the assessment of cognitive and manipulative skills, and simple, clearly defined behaviors. But as *the* solution to the problems of education generally, especially teacher education, it is probably illusion. Proponents of this approach to teacher education argue: The goal of teacher training must be "improved behavior" of the prospective teacher. Logically, then, what is needed is to determine the behaviors one wishes to produce, apply the necessary techniques to produce those behaviors, then test the product to see if the objectives have been achieved. Certainly this would counteract the vagueness often encountered in teacher education and offer a contrast to the worn-out tradition of the lecture course. At least it would force the instructor to ask important questions about his activities.

This concept of accountability is supported by a 100-year-old tradition of behavioristic psychology stretching from the historic experiments by Ivan Pavlov to the recent work of B. F. Skinner and his pupils. Basically, the point of view seeks to modify behavior through manipulation of the stimuli to which a person is exposed or through control of the consequences following the person's behavior. Psychologists using this approach to understanding behavior have been successful in developing a highly efficient technology for behavior modification and their techniques have become widespread to all facets of education.

The Appeal of the Industrial Model

The behavioral objectives approach is also appealing because of its congruence with the industrial-economic model of low-cost, assembly-line efficiency of production that has put this country in the forefront of industrial-technological advancement. Americans are proud of our industrial accomplishments, and it seems only natural to think the same no-nonsense techniques applied to education must reap the same kinds of rewards. Accordingly, extensive efforts are under way to apply systems approaches and industrial management principles to the problems of schooling. Many teachers' colleges are currently experimenting with courses based on the behavioral objectives industrial model. Entire training programs, for example, have been developed, packaged, and shipped to teacher-education institutions across the country.[1] The success of such programs presumably rests on the degree to which the importing institution adopts the package and its specified objectives and follows its prescribed procedures. This is thought to provide "quality assurance." Other institutions use the technical skills approach through various "mini," "micro," or simulated training modules. Such lessons usually start off with a "This-is-how" part, followed by a "Now-you-do-it" phase, and ending with immediate "This-is-how-you-did-it" backfeed which, in turn, leads into the next round. "Behavior modification," "precision teaching," "programed instruction" with hard- and software and similar techniques used in the college classroom are all variations on the behavioral objectives theme.

Operating in the same frame of reference, a number of institutions and state departments of education have begun to establish centers for the development, collection, and "cataloging" of specific teacher competencies. Such catalogs are intended eventually to serve as a "master pool" of effective teacher behaviors. From this the college instructor could extract those that best fit his area of specialty. The competencies would become his course objectives, and, presumably, from then on he would devote his energies and talents to evoking these particular behaviors in his class of students.

Some Limitation of Behavioral Objectives

Because the behavioral objectives approach is firmly anchored in traditional psychology, because it appeals strongly to our sense of practical efficiency, and because it has a certain quality of objectivity and precision, this new approach is in some quarters regarded with a great deal of expectation for success. Some ardent proponents even believe this approach would bring about "a renaissance of American education."[2] Unfortunately, such claims are unrealistic.

The behavioral-objectives performance-based criteria approach to evaluation is consistent with the "Competencies Approach to Teacher Education" we discussed briefly in Chapter I. It represents an essentially closed system of thinking in which ends are all known in advance. It presupposes that what we have come to understand as a teacher's "effectiveness" is the sum total of a series of many discrete events. These events or elements of effectiveness are all known and defined; they only need to be spelled out precisely in terms of measurable behaviors or competencies and taught to education students. In such a system of thinking there is no room for new inputs, for experimentation, pursuit of alternatives, self-exploration, or personal discovery. If the behavioral objectives approach were to be generally adopted or imposed on American education, the effect would be a disproportionate emphasis on ever more finely separated, minutely detailed, and hierarchically ordered specific skills. This would come about at a time when other Western industrialized societies are turning their emphasis in the opposite direction. In a recent survey, for example, one of the authors found that industrialized European countries are increasingly stressing integration of traditional subject matter and learning materials into more embracing, meaningful, life-oriented entities with the purpose of helping students see broad relationships.[3]

Certainly there can be no doubt that behavioral-objectives performance-based criteria approaches to accountability have value. The problem is they are much too limited in scope. When applied to the teaching and learning of precisely defined skills, or to the production of clearly defined simple behavior, the behavioral-objectives model can make important contributions. Applied to the more complex goals and qualities of teacher education, the behavioral-objectives approach is far less satisfactory. As Combs has pointed out in a monograph entitled *Educational Accountability: Beyond Behavioral Objectives*,[4] behavioral objectives are applicable primarily to the simplest and most primitive aspects of the educational endeavor. To assess the complex factors involved in the production of an effective professional helper will call for far more sophisticated techniques. If it is too difficult at present to evaluate teacher-education programs by pupil outcomes, what, then, can we assess?

WHAT CAN BE ASSESSED?

Early in this book we described the effective teacher as a consequence of six conditions:

1. Knowledge of the world and of his subjects.
2. Sensitivity to people, the capacity for empathy.
3. Accurate and appropriate beliefs about people and their behavior.
4. Positive beliefs about self.
5. Appropriate and congruent beliefs about purposes, the goals of society, schools, the classroom, and the teacher's own goals in teaching.
6. The personal discovery of his own appropriate and authentic ways of teaching.

All these can be assessed. Number one, knowledge of subject matter has long been used as a criterion for the success of teacher-education programs. It is what our colleges know how to do best. Clearly we need to have teachers who know their subject fields, and so we will need to continue evaluating success in the degree to which this objective is achieved. But, as we have seen throughout this book, teaching is far more complex than that, and assessment programs will need to deal with the remainder of the list above if we are to avoid a totally distorted picture of our successes and failures.

Items two through six in the list above are not so simply measurable by traditional techniques. They are internal matters having to do with questions of belief, attitudes, purposes, and values that cannot be simply predefined as a set of specific behaviors. As the research on which this book is based has demonstrated, such personal meanings are at the very heart of professional competence.

What goes on in the classroom can only really be understood in terms of what the teacher is trying to do (his purposes) and what the child thinks is happening (his perceptions). Whatever teaching is going on in the classroom will be a consequence of this dynamic interaction. How the situation appears to an outside observer looking on at the process is only descriptive but has only a tenuous relationship to what is *really* happening. What the outside observer thinks is occurring is, after all, irrelevant to what is actually going on. It is the *meanings* of teachers that determine their behavior, and it is these we must seek to assess in determining the effectiveness of a teacher-education program.

The meanings held by educators play a vital role in determining what happens to students everywhere. They provide the basic dynamics from which practices are evolved. They are basic causes of teacher and administrator behavior and determine the nature of what goes on in classrooms and the schools and systems in which they exist. Yet meanings can also be explored, evaluated, and, when necessary, changed. As a consequence, any system of accountability must give the exploration, assessment, and continuous review of educators' purposes an important place in its attempt to help education achieve its fundamental objectives.

The essence of good professional work calls for thinking practitioners able to confront problems and find effective solutions. Often these solutions may be highly unique and incapable of measurement by standard techniques.

Professional responsibility does not demand a prescribed way of behaving. What it does require is that whatever methods are used have the presumption of being good for the client. The emphasis is not on guaranteed outcomes but on the defensible character of what is done. Doctors, for example, are not held responsible for the death of a patient. What they are held responsible for is being able to defend in the eyes of their peers that whatever they did had the presumption of being helpful when applied. Teachers, too, must be prepared to stand this kind of professional scrutiny of their information, beliefs, purposes, and the adequacy of the techniques that they use. Whatever they do should be for a good and sufficient reason, defensible in terms of rational thought, or as a consequence of informal or empirical research. This is an area of accountability sadly overlooked in most educational thinking.

Items two to six in the list of effective teacher characteristics above are essentially matters of meaning. But meanings lie inside people and so are not readily available for measurement by the techniques with which we are most familiar. They can, however, be assessed. Indeed, the research on which this book is based did precisely that.

THE ASSESSMENT OF PERSONAL MEANING

Since meanings lie inside persons, at first glance it would seem impossible to assess them. It is true that meanings cannot be observed directly, but neither can electricity, and we have managed to measure that effectively by inference. The same thing works for personal meaning. While meanings cannot be read directly, they can be inferred by a process of "reading behavior backward." If it is true that behavior is the product of perception, then it should be possible to observe a person's behavior and infer the nature of the perceptions that produced it. Such assessment calls for human judgment, a characteristic currently regarded with suspicion and disdain by accountability "experts." What a pity! Human judgment is what we must use at every phase of our normal existence. The improvement of human judgment is what education is all about. The very essence of good teaching is the intelligent, creative use of human judgment.

The objective methods of science provide us with important checks on human observation and with logical presumption of greater accuracy when we use such checks. Yet human judgment is all we have to depend on in the absence of objective devices. We cannot shrink from confronting our pressing problems for lack of precision tools. We must do what we can with what we have. Persons who never used judgment would be forever confined to what was immediately palpable and observable. Judgment frees us to go beyond mere observation. To reject it as a tool for assessment is to limit ourselves to the least important aspects of our educational effort and so to assure the increasing irrelevance of a system already desperately ill of that disease.

The belief that judgment is somehow unscientific is an illusion. All science, of whatever description, is dependent on human judgment. Science itself is merely a device to refine and control human judgment. The goal is not its elimination but its effective and efficient use. Judgment requires the use of the "observer-as-instrument" and, of course, this instrument, like any other in scientific use, must be properly calibrated to make sure its readings are as reliable as we can possibly make them. That can be done. The physical scientist relies on one or more of six important tests of validity:

1. Feelings of subjective certainty.
2. Conformity with known facts.
3. Mental manipulation.
4. Predictive power.
5. Social agreement.
6. Internal consistency.

The process of inferring meaning calls for a holistic rather than an atomistic approach to understanding human behavior. Instead of cataloging specific behaviors, the observer uses himself as an observation instrument and observes all he can by immersing himself in the situation. By a continuous process of observing, inferring, and testing his inferences over and over, he is able in time to arrive at accurate understandings of the peculiar meanings producing the behavior in the persons he is observing. Meanings can be assessed.

The problem is not one of learning to do something entirely new. It is a matter of learning to do what all of us already do occasionally with persons who are important to us. We have little trouble being sensitive to and interpretive of meanings existing for those above us in the hierarchy, such as principals, supervisors, and superintendents. What is needed now is to learn to do these things more often, more precisely, and in more disciplined fashion with persons in positions subservient to us, such as students. These are skills that can be learned. Indeed, many fine teachers already have them.

If such procedures for assessing meaning seem imprecise and vague as we have described them here, they need not be. It is possible to make inferences with high degrees of accuracy and reliability by application of the usual tests for scientific credibility. Inferential techniques are already widely used in psychological research, especially in the study of such personal meanings as attitudes, beliefs, self-concept, and purposes. The assessment of meaning outcomes of education can be made with whatever degree of precision is desired, from informal observation to highly controlled and systematized procedures.

The assessment of meaning has an additional advantage. It focuses the attention of educators on the causes of behavior directly. The attempt to catalog behaviors with too great specificity may actually take us further and further away from the basic meanings producing them.

Assessment of personal meaning is not only likely to be more effective, it has additional advantages of great practical value. It is far simpler for teachers at any level to manage than highly specific lists of behavioral objectives because there are fewer concepts to master. Attention can be given to basic principles rather than to limitless details. The teacher preoccupied with manipulating behavior is likely to find himself dealing with problems through such controlling devices as coercion, exhortation, bribery, and such approaches are very likely to produce their own resistance in the students whose behavior he is attempting to change. It is a part of our American heritage to resist being managed, and it should not surprise us if such techniques call forth in students ingenious and creative devices for sabotaging the system.

The teacher who is concerned about personal meanings of students is much more likely to find that his relationships with students are warmer and more human. Human aspects are not rejected but actively sought and appreciated. Empathic teachers, honestly concerned with understanding how students think, feel, and perceive are far more likely than other teachers to be liked by their students, have less problems with motivation and discipline, find themselves more successful in carrying out their assigned tasks—to say nothing of being more relaxed and happy on the job.

DETERMINING OUTCOMES OF A TEACHER-EDUCATION PROGRAM

Innumerable possibilities exist for the evaluation of teacher-education programs and, of course, this book is not the place for a detailed description of such techniques. So much information is needed that all avenues of exploration should be employed wherever possible. Both objective and inferential approaches to assessment need to be utilized to provide us with the kinds of information each way of examining the problem can bring to light. Thousands of studies bearing on the evaluation of teachers in traditional ways have now been published and the interested reader is referred to those for more comprehensive information. Research studies designed to explore teacher meanings are far fewer, but, as a beginning, interested readers may wish to explore some of the references in the footnotes below.[5–15]

SOME INITIAL RESEARCH FINDINGS ON THE FLORIDA PROGRAM

As one example of an attempt to explore a teacher-education program from both external and internal approaches, we present below some of the findings of follow-up research on the Florida Experimental Program. It also seems appropriate to close this book with a small indication of what the research showed when the kind of program advocated in this volume was actually placed in effect.

A U.S. Department of Education grant made it possible to follow up on thirty-five graduates in the spring of 1972 by actually sending trained observers into their classrooms. Information was also obtained from a control group from the regular program who had graduated in 1970-71. Teams of observers spent approximately one day in each classroom using two distinct approaches to the evaluation of the teachers: (1) a perceptual-inferential approach, and (2) a behavioral-observation approach. In the first approach the teachers' perceptions were inferred from classroom observations and recorded on the Perceptual Dimensions Scale (PDS) developed by Combs and others in a series of basic researches on effective helpers.[5] The dimensions on the PDS are:

1. Internal-External Frame of Reference.
2. Perceptions of Others as Able or Unable.
3. Perceptions of Self as Adequate or Inadequate.
4. Perceptions of Self as Revealing or Concealing.
5. Perceptions of Purpose as Freeing or Controlling.
6. Perceptions of Goals as Larger or Smaller.

Using the behavioral approach two observation systems were used: (1) the Teacher Practices Observation Record (TPOR), developed by Bob Burton Brown.[6] This instrument is based on Dewey's experimentalism and measures experimental or nonexperimental teaching; (2) the Reciprocal Category System (RCS), a modification of Flanders' 10-category System of Interaction Analysis.[7] This system is basically concerned with verbal behaviors associated with positive social climate. This project focused on the following dimensions[18]:

(a) Warm-Cool.
(b) Accept-Correct.
(c) Amplify-Direct.
(d) Elicit-Initiate.

Thus, in the internal approach observers inferred the teachers' meanings or perceptions, while in the external approach the observers recorded either the presence or the frequencies of certain behaviors as specified.

The development of appropriate positive perceptions, beliefs, and attitudes about self, others, goals, and purposes are primary objectives of the experimental program. The research therefore predicted that experimental teachers would score significantly more positively on the Perceptional Dimensions Scale. The results summarized in Table 10–1 supports that hypothesis. As can be noted, the experimental teachers had a significantly higher total score on the perceptual dimensions than did the control teachers. Most particularly, they perceived others as able and possessed larger rather than smaller goals to a significantly higher degree. In addition they tended to see themselves as more adequate and were more self-revealing.

When the perceptual ratings were examined more closely, important differences between our experimental teachers and the control group in the proportion of extreme negative and positive ratings appeared. As indicated in figures

TABLE 10–1. Mean Distribution of Scores on the Perceptual Dimensions Scale

Perceptual Dimensions	Experimental Group $\bar{X}$	Experimental Group SD	Control Group $\bar{X}$	Control Group SD	df = 63 F-ratio
1. Internal-External Reference	3.22	1.33	3.66	1.60	1.448
2. Others Able —Unable	3.22	1.30	4.06	1.55	5.589*
3. Self Adequate—Inadequate	2.88	1.18	3.43	1.30	3.149
4. Revealing—Concealing	3.42	1.44	4.13	1.50	3.716
5. Freeing—Controlling	3.71	1.52	4.26	1.59	2.030
6. Goals Larger —Smaller	3.17	1.40	3.90	1.42	4.209*
7. Total Score	19.66	7.42	23.47	7.71	4.101*

*$p \leq .01$

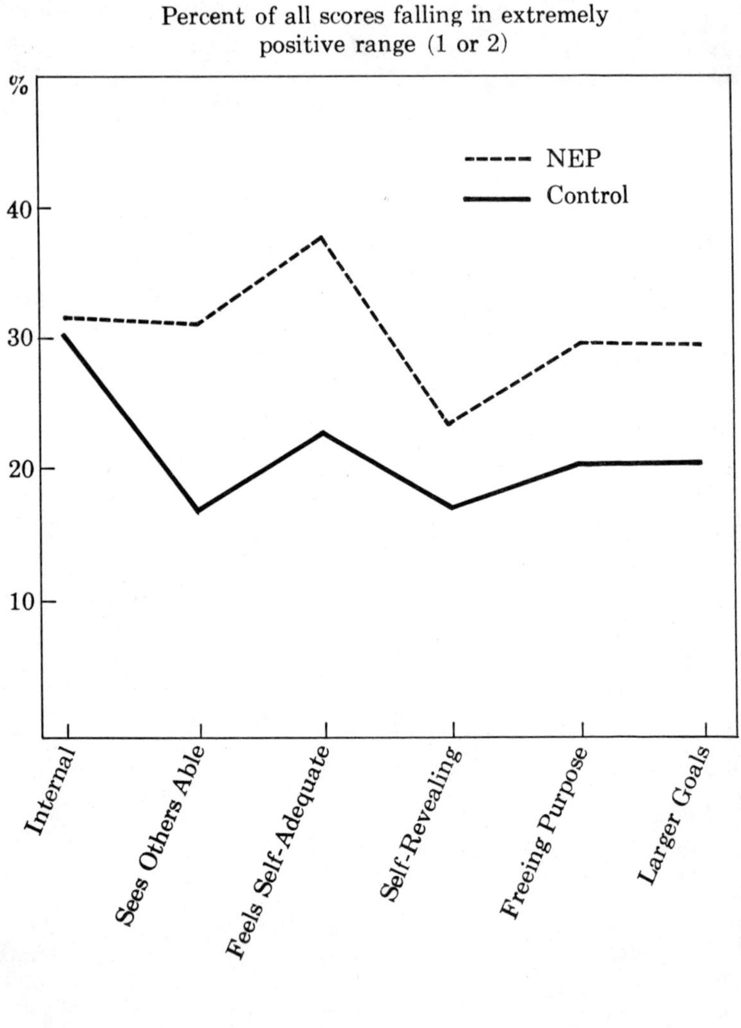

FIGURE 10–1

10-1 and 10-2, a smaller proportion of experimental teachers received extremely negative perceptual scores (6–7), while a larger proportion were rated at the extreme positive end (1–2) of the PDS.

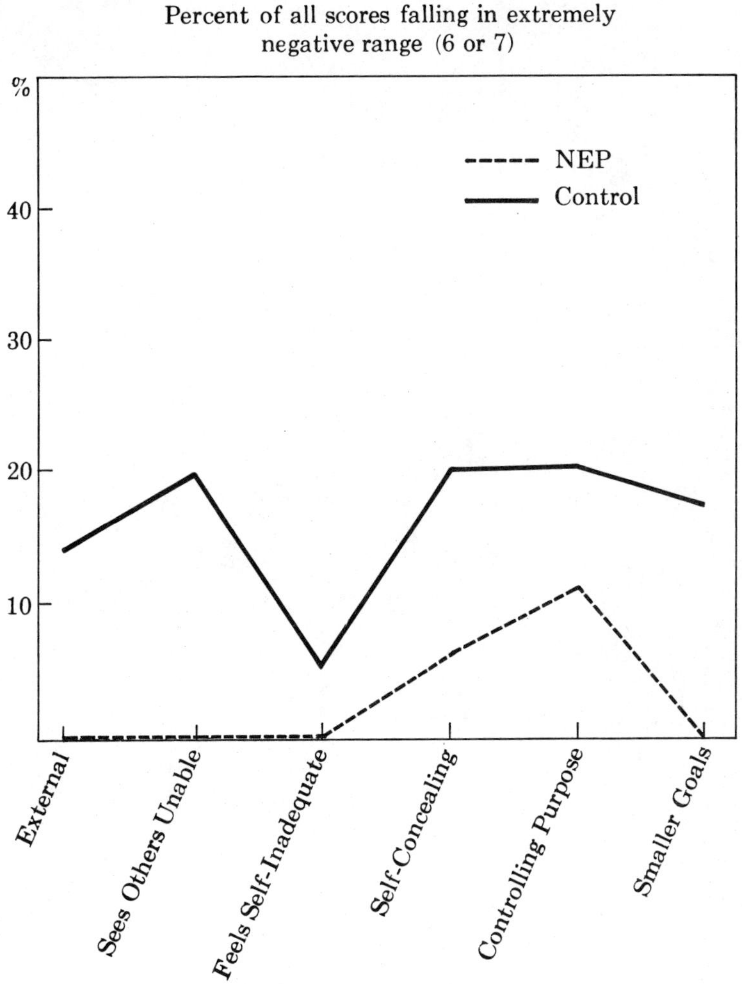

FIGURE 10–2

Results of the systematic behavior observations are summarized in Table 10–2.

It can be seen that the experimental group more often showed positive climate-producing verbal interactions (RCS)

TABLE 10–2. Mean Distribution of Observations on Two Systems of Behavior Observation

	Reciprocal Category System Exp. Group	Control Group	
Categories	$\overline{X}$	$\overline{X}$	F-ratio
1. Teacher Warms	50.49	49.42	.182
11. Student Warms	50.03	49.92	.005
2. Teacher Accepts	48.71	52.09	1.442
12. Student Accepts	50.33	49.62	.078
3. Teacher Amplifies	51.32	50.99	.076
13. Student Amplifies	51.20	51.52	.022
4. Teacher Elicits	50.24	52.70	1.231
14. Student Initiates	51.11	48.70	1.142

	Teacher Practices Observation Record Exp. Group	Control Group	
	$\overline{X}$	$\overline{X}$	t
Even-Numbered Items	1,631.52	1,545.68	3.51*
Factors	$\overline{X}$	$\overline{X}$	F-ratio
1. Pupil Freedom	104.28	99.80	.4173*
2. Exp. Teaching	265.47	260.61	.4915*
3. Nonexp. Tchg.	147.77	147.72	.0002
4. Teacher-Centered Right Answer Focus	201.77	212.43	4.2127*

*P ≤ .01

although not at statistically significant levels. In their overall classroom practices, experimental teaching (TPOR) was apparent to a significantly greater extent in the NEP teachers than in the control group. Among the four factored dimensions on the TPOR, NEP teachers were significantly lower on factor 6 indicating a less teacher-centered/right-answer focus than the control group.

An on the job follow-up research on NEP students inquiring into their feelings about their professional education a year after graduation shows they feel their preparation gave them greater confidence, more skill in helping others develop, and more opportunities for self-initiated experiences when compared with a control group from the regular program.

A great deal of follow-up research yet needs to be done to properly assess the NEP program. From the data so far available, however, it is evident the program has much merit and seems to support the perceptual approach to teacher education outlined in this book.

ENDNOTES

[1]Herbert J. Klausmeier, "Educational Research: From the R. & D. Centers into Practice," *Educational Leadership* (April 1972): 598–601.

[2]Leon Lessinger and Dwight Allen, "Performance Proposals for Educational Funding: A New Approach to Federal Resource Allocation," *Phi Delta Kappan* 51, no. 3 (November 1969): 136–37.

[3]Hannelore Wass, "Educational Accountability Here and Abroad," *Educational Leadership* (April 1972): 618–620.

[4]Arthur W. Combs, *Educational Accountability: Beyond Behavioral Objectives* (Washington, D.C.: Association for Supervision and Curriculum Development, 1972).

[5]A. W. Combs, "Florida Studies in the Helping Professions," Social Science Monograph no. 37 (Gainsville: University of Florida Press, 1969).

[6]Robert G. Brown, "A Study of the Perceptual Organization of Elementary and Secondary 'Outstanding Young Educators,' " Unpublished Doctoral Dissertation (Gainsville: University of Florida, 1970).

[7]Chunghoon Choy, "The Relationship of College Teacher Effectiveness to Conceptual Systems of Orientation and Perceptual Orientation," Unpublished Doctoral Dissertation (Greeley, Colorado: University of Northern Colorado, 1969)

[8]Charles V. L. Dedrick, "The Relationship Between Perceptual Characteristics and Effective Teaching at the Junior College Level," Unpublished Doctoral Dissertation (Gainsville: University of Florida, 1972).

[9]Donald A. Dellow, "A Study of the Perceptual Organization of the Teachers and Conditions of Empathy, Congruence, and Positive Regard," Unpublished Doctoral Dissertation (Gainsville: University of Florida, March, 1971).

[10]Eunice J. Doyle, "The Relationship Between College Teacher Effectiveness and Inferred Characteristics of the Adequate Personality," Unpublished Doctoral Dissertation (Greeley, Colorado: University of Northern Colorado, 1969).

[11]Robert E. Morgenstern, "The Relationship Between Two Modes of Interpersonal Conditions and College Teacher Effectiveness," Unpublished Doctoral Dissertation (Greeley, Colorado: University of Northern Colorado, 1969).

[12]Lois P. Picht, "Self-Concept in Relation to Effectiveness in Student Teaching," Unpublished Doctoral Dissertation (Greeley, Colorado: University of Northern Colorado, 1969).

[13]Richard Harold Usher, "The Relationship of Perceptions of Self, Others, and the Helping Task to Certain Measures of College Faculty Effectiveness," Unpublished Doctoral Dissertation (Gainsville: University of Florida, 1966).

[14]Richard Usher and John Hanke, "Third Force in Psychology and College Teacher Effectiveness Research at the University of Northern Colorado," *Colorado Journal of Educational Research* 10, no. 2 (Winter 1971).

[15]Herman G. Vonk, "The Relationship of Teacher Effectiveness to Perception of Self and Teaching Purposes," Unpublished Doctoral Dissertation (Gains ville: University of Florida, June, 1970).

[16]Bob Burton Brown, *The Experimental Mind in Education* (New York. Harper and Row, 1968).

[17]Ned A. Flanders, *Teacher Influence, Pupil Attitudes, and Achievement* (Washington, D.C., Cooperative Research Program OE–25040, 1965).

[18]Richard L. Ober, Ernest Bentley, and Edith Miller, *Systematic Observatior in the Classroom* (Englewood Cliffs, N. J.: Prentice-Hall, 1971).

Index

D

E

F

G

H

I

O

P

Q

R

S